MW00799882

# THE
# HOW
## AND
# WOW
## OF
# TEACHING

Kathy Paterson

Pembroke Publishers Limited

*Dedicated to Emma—she is the wow!*

I would like to thank the following people for their help, support, and amazing ideas. Without them, the writing of this book would not have been possible.

Stacy Fysh, Principal of Glenora
    Elementary school, EPSB
Jason Wyatt, Teacher, Parkland
    School Division #70, Alberta
Mary Macchiusi, publisher, wise
    supporter, Forever Friend
Kat Mototsune, editor
    extraordinaire
Emma Paterson, granddaughter

© **2019 Pembroke Publishers**
538 Hood Road
Markham, Ontario, Canada L3R 3K9
www.pembrokepublishers.com

All rights reserved.
No part of this publication may be reproduced in any form or by any means electronic or mechanical, including photocopy, scanning, recording, or any information, storage or retrieval system, without permission in writing from the publisher. Excerpts from this publication may be reproduced under licence from Access Copyright, or with the express written permission of Pembroke Publishers Limited, or as permitted by law.

Every effort has been made to contact copyright holders for permission to reproduce borrowed material. The publishers apologize for any such omissions and will be pleased to rectify them in subsequent reprints of the book.

Funded by the Government of Canada
Financé par le gouvernement du Canada | **Canadä**  ONTARIO CREATES

**Library and Archives Canada Cataloguing in Publication**

Title: The how and wow of teaching : quick ideas for mastering any classroom situation effectively, efficiently, and enthusiastically / Kathy Paterson.

Names: Paterson, Kathy, author.

Identifiers: Canadiana (print) 20190153415 | Canadiana (ebook) 20190153423 | ISBN 9781551383422 (softcover) | ISBN 9781551389417 (PDF)

Subjects: LCSH: Effective teaching.

Classification: LCC LB1025.3 .P38 2019 | DDC 371.3—dc23

Editor: Kat Mototsune
Cover Design: John Zehethofer
Typesetting: Jay Tee Graphics Ltd.

Printed and bound in Canada
9 8 7 6 5 4 3 2 1

**FSC**
www.fsc.org
**MIX**
Paper from
responsible sources
FSC® C004071

# Contents

# Introduction

Another book about teaching?

Why this book?

Will it wow me?

What does it offer that I can't get from Google?

These are valid questions that require valid answers. What this book can do for you is save time and frustration, facilitate your teaching experiences, generally make each day a little easier, and, at the same time, help you create wow in your classroom. The wow factor is that element that captures students' attention and enhances experience—something every teacher hopes to accomplish. When teachers teach effectively, efficiently, and enthusiastically, as opposed to simply instructing, both they and their charges will experience the wow! But as every educator knows, it's not always easy to teach with passion, especially when the *how* of the profession is sometimes not clear. *The How and Wow of Teaching* will bring together these two elements so that great teachers can become even greater, and also can get profound satisfaction from their work. In other words, this book endeavors to provide both the how and the wow to facilitate the highest level of teaching and learning.

Since the wow of teaching is a direct result of understanding the how of teaching, how is it possible to make all the magic, all that wow, come about in your class? And how do you do that while managing the endless requirements of your profession? The answer is that you find resources like this book, keep them handy, and love what you do.

Internet searches, as productive as they might be, take time, skill, energy, and the ability to weed out the not-so-good from the good, and then the time to tabulate, collate, and record. Rather than using your valuable time in this sort of search, you can access instantly available ideas from this book. For example, you can use an Inaccurate Analogy (page 9) to begin a lesson, or you can play Yes, Yes, No! (page 81) to improve spelling. Both you and your students will enjoy the inherent wow of these activities.

Consider the following:

Teacher A is fresh out of teacher training. She enters the school on Day One filled with excitement and zeal, her arms overflowing with books, papers, charts, and various other supplies. She greets her fresh-faced new students and prepares to begin her very first lesson and… she suddenly realizes she is not sure how to start. Day One is filled with hesitancy and very little, if any, wow.

Teacher B has experience. She has been in the profession for several years and feels confident she knows many of the tricks of the trade. She enters the school on Day One carrying a single book and wearing a confident smile. She greets her students and prepares to deliver her beginning-of-the-year lesson and… she suddenly thinks to herself, *This is exactly how I began last year, and all the years before that.*

*Perhaps it's time for something new.* Day One begins with some wow, as the excitement of getting reacquainted with peers and students is high, but fades considerably as the teacher falls back into the comfortable, established pattern of how.

In both these cases, the what and why of teaching is being handled by teacher training and/or experience. However, the how of the profession often is not as evident; although experienced teachers will have developed many teaching techniques already, they might also sometimes need the motivational boost fresh ideas can provide. Since wow comes naturally with bold and original how, it, too, can easily be lost.

The job of teaching today is more important than ever before because teachers provide the humanity that technology can never supply. Thus, teachers need hands-on toolboxes filled with readily usable how-to ideas that will quickly enable them to do everything in the classroom, from opening a lesson to closing the day, and do it with such ease, confidence, and pizzazz that the wow factor is always evident.

Teaching how-tos don't come automatically with an education degree. Neither do they remain stagnant; they continually require updating, reviewing, and refining. This is why teachers attend conferences and professional development days, which are great shots in the arm. But these resources are intermittent and you, the teacher, still need to deal with the day-to-day teaching and managing of your classroom. This book will help you do that and save you considerable time and effort.

In this book, you will find a cornucopia of ideas—practical and concrete suggestions, in easy-to-use point form—to facilitate teaching throughout the year. With the variety and freshness of these ideas, the wow factor will ever be present. In addition there are hints, quotes, and How-to-Wow summaries to keep you moving ahead with poise and pride. The chapters address various aspects of teaching—lesson planning, teaching the curriculum, teaching strategies, strategies for life and living, and other teaching responsibilities—by outlining the how and then focusing on particular ways to increase the wow factor.

Without new ideas, teaching can be overwhelming, inordinately time-consuming, and most certainly less effective. Even those of you who have been in the profession for years may find yourself in a rut; you need some fresh wowful ideas, some new how-to-teach hints. Given the amount of time you need and want to spend with your students, and the fast pace of our world today, there is little left for researching, collecting, or experimenting with ideas that don't work. This book does the work for you.

Teaching is fun! Allow me to help keep it that way.

**Teaching is much more than a profession; it is a lifestyle. And teachers are among the privileged few who have been allocated the responsibility of protecting the past and preparing for the future.**

# Chapter 1 Lesson Planning

Every teacher has had the disappointing experience of a lesson that bombs. For whatever reason, students either were not engaged or simply didn't get it. Changing a less-than-effective lesson into one that roars can move teaching from mediocre to wow!

## Starting and Stopping a Lesson, and Everything in Between

Not all lessons are pre-planned; many are spontaneous teachable moments. For prepped lessons, concise, snappy, attention-getting beginnings; enthusiastic deliveries; and succinct, recapping closings are the tenets of good teaching. A good lesson opening will not require a lot of pre-thought or a lot of time at the lesson onset, but will help ensure the success of the lesson. Similarly, an organized, engaging delivery of the information, as well as a definite closing, will help both you and your students to be successful

### Beginning a Lesson

Not every lesson will have a motivating opening; teachers are extremely busy and often have to rely on what is suggested by teachers guides or curricula. However, if you want to make a lesson truly memorable, a snappy opening will help you do that. When you begin your career as a teacher you will not have the time to assemble your own personal list of effective openings. In truth, seasoned teachers don't have time to create new or original openings, and often depend on old favorites. The following list can help you expand your repertoire of lesson openings.

### Question

**When Napoleon Bonaparte said that "why" and "how" are words so important that they cannot be too often used, he was alluding to the power of questioning.**

Ask a pertinent question, the answer to which will lead directly to the upcoming lesson. Avoid questions that lead to yes/no responses and allow a few minutes to discuss all responses before directing students to your lesson objective. Some examples:

*Who has watched the night sky?*
*If you have ever run into trouble at/when/during.... Raise your hand if you have.*
*What would you do if...?*
*Raise your hand if you've ever seen/thought/felt/wondered/heard....*

## Visual

Share an engaging picture or other visual. Display it for a few moments before saying anything, allowing students time to formulate their own ideas, then ask a leading question or simply invite discussion. Some visuals you can use:

- photograph
- computer image
- screen saver
- calendar page
- poster
- cartoon

## Anecdote

Students love stories—real or imaginary—especially if they involve you! They have a natural curiosity about their teacher and will listen intently to any recounting of your adventures. These can be entirely made-up or factual (depending on how much personal information you care to reveal). The more humorous the story, the more motivating it is for students. They enjoy seeing their teacher as a real person. Of course, the anecdote can be about anyone, but the closer the main character is to the students, the better. The yarn should, of course, lead to your lesson objective. Examples include:

- a tale about losing something for a lesson on organization
- a tale about a strange plant growing in your garden for a lesson on ecosystems
- a tale about a dream you had about anything related to your topic

## Object

Be creative; look around your home and/or room with a critical eye for any object that is both interesting and easily manipulated and stored. Hold the object out for all to see and remain silent for a few moments to allow students to think about why you are displaying it. You can then ask them directly why they think you are showing the object or ask a leading question that directs thinking to your lesson objective. A supply of viable objects you keep in your desk for instant use might include

- a pencil for a lesson about trees
- a piece of fruit for a lesson in science, health, social studies
- a small figurine or toy for a lesson in social studies or whatever the figure represents
- any classroom item, such as a stapler, for a lesson in science, art, etc.
- a string of beads for a lesson in math
- a small purse or bag for a lesson in science, or creative writing ("What's hidden inside?")

## Action

Students of all ages need to move! Ask students to stand up without giving a reason, then lead them through a series of movements you can relate to your lesson objective. In fact, even if you cannot directly connect the actions to your lesson, you can force the connection by saying something like "Now that we've shaken off some restless energy, we are going to take a look at…" Possible movements:

- *Shake every body part* for a science lesson on compounds
- *Stretch high/low* for a lesson on math measurement
- *Run on the spot* for a lesson in health, history
- *Clap high/low/to the side* for a lesson on writing (applauding a good author)
- *Wrap arms around body tightly and wiggle* for a science lesson on cocoons

## Inaccurate Analogy

Share a quick, ridiculous yarn about something you present as being the same as, or similar to, something related to your lesson objective, but for which the relationship is obviously wrong. For example, you might say "We all know that an apple is a lot like our heads, right?" as a lead to a lesson about various fruits and vegetables and classification. When students disagree, you can readily lead the discussion to what apples are really *like*. Possible analogy ideas include

- Comparing a specific animal to some inanimate object for a science lesson
- Comparing verbs to nouns ("We know that verbs are just like nouns.") for a lesson in reading/writing
- Comparing mathematical concepts to painting a picture ("We use numbers to create a colorful picture.") for a lesson on addition/subtraction/multiplication/division

## Silly Sentence

Similar to the inaccurate analogy, a silly sentence is amusing because of either its content or the way it is delivered. As teachers, we should always be willing to mix a little silly into every day. Think of a sentence related to your lesson objective and say it in the silliest way possible:

- Make it a tongue-twister and invite students to repeat it.
- Sing it like opera, in country-music style, or as rock or rap.
- Mix up the order of the words and invite students to make sense of what you are saying.
- Delivery it in a chanting manner while marching.
- Drum on your desk while speaking.
- Clap, shake your hands, or wave your hands in the air after each word in the sentence.

## Open-Ended Statement

Tell students you are going to play a quick word game. The word "game" always catches attention! Invite them to shout out quick endings to sentences that relate to your lesson objective but could be completed in various ways. After a couple of minutes of this, repeat the sentences with correct endings and see how close the students got to the truth. For example, open-ended statements for a lesson on summarizing:

When we put ideas together we end up with a _____ (*summary*)
Key points can be made into a _____ (*summary*)

---

**"We see in order to move; we move in order to see." — William Gibson. This summarizes beautifully the objective of this strategy. In moving, students see the lesson's intention.**

**"If people did not sometimes do silly things, nothing intelligent would ever get done." — Ludwig Wittgenstein**

Things you read for information or pleasure can be _____ (*summarized*)

A short form can be called a _____ (*summary*)

## Word-Connect Game

As always, the word "game" is motivating and can lead quickly to your lesson objective. Tell students you are going to "bat words around as if they were ping-pong balls." Offer a word and have them spontaneously throw back whatever words first come to mind. Of course, the words you present will all be related to your lesson objective. After a few minutes of the game, go back to your list of words and explain how they connect to the lesson.

1. Tell students their job is to respond as quickly as possible to your word cue by saying out loud (not shouting) the first word that comes to mind, then responding in the same way to the words said in response.
2. Model by offering "red" as the cue, to which you model responses: "apple," then "fruit," then "banana."
3. Point out the connection between the words, and how one word led naturally to the next.
4. Provide cue words related to the lesson objective.
5. Stop the dialogue after a few minutes and debrief by looking at the connections.

For example, words related to a lesson on mathematical fractions might include

- *parts*
- *pies*
- *divide*
- *reducing*
- *whole*
- *cutting*

Examples of words related to a language arts lesson might include

- *write*
- *protagonist*
- *setting*
- *conclusion*
- *simile*

Examples of words related to a social studies lesson might include

- *community*
- *history*
- *friendship*
- *responsibility*
- *laws*

## Teacher as Actor

This is a form of the game charades. In this game, you are the actor. Simply act our a scene/situation/person that relates to your lesson. All teachers are, by the very nature of their profession, actors. You are aware of your audience, you know how to project and hold the attention of your audience—you are an actor! But if you feel uncomfortable handling this, secretly (in the hall, in writing) invite a student to do the acting for you.

"Never miss a good chance to shut up." — Will Rogers

1. Tell students an actor is going to portray a scene for them and they are to guess what is going on. They must not speak until the actor is finished.
2. Silently act out your lesson objective scene.
3. Debrief and connect the scene to your lesson objectives.

The following are possible examples of scenes to act:

- become a character from history for a lesson in social studies
- be a plant "growing" for a science (biology) lesson
- use fingers and body parts to illustrate mathematical concepts
- run on the spot for a lesson in health or physics
- be an animal for a science lesson
- act like a robot or automaton for a coding lesson

## Joke

I encourage the purchase of an actual book. Of course there are many jokes available online, but nothing beats a book for convenience and quick access.

Anything that starts with a quick joke is a winner. One-liners work the most effectively; for example, *What do you get when you plant kisses in the ground? Tulips!* This joke could easily open a science lesson, a health lesson, a math lesson (e.g., *If I plant 6 seeds and get 2 tulips from each, how many tulips do I have?*), or any lesson relating to feelings (humor), etc. Find a good children's joke book; I like *Highlight's Best Kids' Jokes Ever*.

## Planned Mistake

This is one of my favorite ways to open a lesson, as it requires no preparation or even pre-thought on the part of the teacher. Simply select a small part of your upcoming lesson and offer it to students in an obviously incorrect manner. As teachers, we are very aware that mistakes and failures are instructive. Only by trying to learn from mistakes can we move forward toward success. This is an important truth to reinforce with students all the time, and this particular lesson-initiating strategy helps to do that while it motivates for the upcoming goal. Students will be quick to point out the mistake, and you go from there. One teacher I know (Jason Wyatt) likes to start a science lesson with a bald-faced lie and an invitation to students to prove him wrong. He once created a company called Carbon Cycle and told his students it was a bicycle company whose use of composite carbon monobonded fibre in the construction of their frames makes the bikes stand up to the rigors of BMX racing. Some of his Grade 7 students believed it because they trusted information that "sounded smart and used big words." The class spent a double block disproving the teacher's statement and discussing the importance of critical thinking and fact checking. So you might want to try an absolute lie, or even a slight mistake:

- spell/say/read/enunciate a word incorrectly for any language arts lesson
- write a math problem on the board and solve it incorrectly
- make an incorrect verbal statement about your lesson objective. For example you might say, "Today we are going to take a look at ecosystems, just like nurses and doctors do in their work," or "We will be looking at color blending in art, to create muffins." The more ridiculous the statement, the better.

- demonstrate a skill poorly and incorrectly for a lesson in physical education, science
- emphasize that you will be discussing creative writing, then write a very basic sentence on the board (e.g., *The boy walks.*); ask students if they like it, and why/why not

### Riddle

Opening with a riddle gets minds working and students interested. It serves as a great conversation piece, and wakes up students' wonder, problem-solving, and collaborative work. Riddles encourage using alternate meanings of words, and searching for key words that will solve them.

Thanks to Jason Wyatt for this one.

1. Have the riddle posted large when students come into room, labeled Riddle of the Day.
2. Allow about 5 minutes of free talk to figure out the riddle.
3. Present the lesson objective and see if students can tie the riddle, or any part of it, to the objective. This might not always work, but it's stimulating and thought-provoking.

## The Delivery TRAIN

There is an acronym that can help you frame a lesson and save time in planning. The delivery of the lesson can be summarized and remembered by the acronym TRAIN. It reminds you that you are going to train your students, or, if a touch of humor gets you going, helps you of yourself as a train forging ahead with direction and purpose.

### T = Teach

Once students have become engaged, it is time for the purpose of the lesson to be revealed. This is the first step in lesson delivery, and in teaching. It consists primarily of sharing the lesson objective(s) in a manner students will understand and relate to. It is a summary of the knowledge, understanding, and/or skills students will have at the end of the lesson. There is considerable data available about lesson objectives, but perhaps the best thing to remember is that students must understand exactly what is expected of them. For example: *At the end of this lesson you will be able to make a _____, or understand _____, or solve _____.*

Lesson objectives will be based on the curriculum but broken down into manageable components for students. The objective could be an explanation of how the learning will be necessary for further learning to take place; e.g., *You need to understand how to _____ before we can move on to_____. I will show you how.* Take a few seconds to share your objectives with the students then move on to delivery the lesson.

I cannot stress enough how important enthusiasm is to the main component of teaching, effective delivery of your lesson. Think back to any public speaker you have encountered—a professor, a spiritual leader, a politician. What made you tune in or tune out? The excitement and zeal of the speaker's voice, content, and general appearance make a world of difference.

"The secret of genius is to carry the spirit of the child into old age, which means never losing your enthusiasm." — Aldous Huxley

Put all you can into your lesson delivery; be the genius teacher you know you can be:

- Use voice intonations, cadence, intensity, loudness, and softness.
- Be very aware of body language (nonverbal communication) and make it match the enthusiasm in your voice. Be animated!
- Use props whenever you can. These can be anything within your sight— simply think *appeal to the senses*. For example, a pencil from your desk could be an example of a tree end-product, something sharp, a conical shape, a tool, etc.

### R = Review

While reviews can be integrated with lesson delivery (e.g., minireviews as you go), they should also occur at the end of the actual providing of information. Make the review simple and concise. At this point you review *for* the students; you will expect them to create their own closures in the next step. Use phrases like these:

*I just demonstrated how to...*
*We have been learning...*
*Now that we know how to _____, we will be able to _____.*
*Basically, I have been talking about/sharing/showing you/revealing...*

### A = Access

This refers to checking for understanding, to accessing the level of success of your lesson. You need to see how much students have absorbed, what they are confused about, where areas of strengths and weaknesses lie, etc. The best way to access is to question. Avoid questions that lead to yes/no responses, instead wording your questions to promote thought and comprehension. Of course, the questions will differ according to what skill, attitude, or understanding you are teaching, and wording is always important. Use questions like these:

- *Can you summarize for me what you just learned? Jot the points in your _____.*
- *What are ten words that relate to what we were just discussing/doing/ thinking?*
- *With a neighbor, ask each other a good question about what we were just doing. Be prepared to share your questions with the rest of the class.*
- *What did you just learn? Raise your hand and share.*

### I = Involve

At this point, it is necessary to involve students in some sort of activity that will reinforce the learning and provide practice and/or extended thought. Teachers are experts at this; workbooks, creative handouts, and questions are all Involve activities, but perhaps there are a few more creative ideas:

- Let students know where they will go from here, i.e., what comes next, as well as how/where they might use the information/skill/attitude in their own lives.

- Ask students to share one word, idea, or thought about the lesson with a neighbor.
- Have them write a brief answer to parents' proverbial question, "What did you learn in school today?"; they include something specific from the particular lesson.
- Invite students to create a student-designed pop quiz. Have them create three quick response questions for use in a future class.
- Have students draw a sketch/chart/diagram/outline/etc. using information from the lesson.

## N = Note

"Memory is a magnet. It will pull to it and hold only material nature has designed it to attract." — Jessamyn West
It is doubtful that the tiny elements of what made your lesson good or not so good can be considered material nature has designed to be attractive to memory, so use the strategy of immediately jotting down a few salient notes post lesson.

The final step in the delivery of an excellent lesson is to take personal notes that indicate to yourself the success or failure of your lesson. These should be quick points to remind yourself of pertinent information. Remember that your busy brain is full and, even though you intend to remember those facts, chances are they will evaporate if you don't record them now.

- Always have handy a notebook and pen. Instant access of this makes the Note step much easier. If you can't immediately see a medium for recording instant jot notes, you will not record them. You do not have time to seek and find.
- Train yourself to be a 30-Second Thought person. In 30 seconds you can jot down a few words that will suffice to remind you later about the pros/cons of the lesson.
- Avoid thinking, *I'll do it later/at break/at lunchtime.* You won't! Something else will push to the head of the line of important things to do and it will be forgotten. Do it now!

Review your jot notes at the end of the day. Allow only five minutes for this. If you know it's only going to take five minutes, you can make it happen. Most likely your notes won't require anything other than a quick reminder for yourself. For instance, my jot notes after a writing class were simply *More stimulus.* This reminded me that, for the writing class the following day, I needed to have a few more visuals available before students began. They were writing descriptive sentences based on calendar-page images, but some of the boys were not at all interested in the pages I had chosen. The next day I brought another calendar (with animals), as my jot notes had suggested. Of course, it is possible that you are a better jot-notetaker than I am, and you take more detailed notes. Keep in mind that this needs to be a time-practical task, because it falls right in the middle of your otherwise full day.

Ask yourself the following questions or, for time efficiency, create a chart or fill-in sheet that presents points so you can simply check or mark X:

- how successful the lesson was on a scale of 1 (perfect) to 3 (not so perfect). Keep the scale short and simple.
- what needs more time/work/review
- where to go next
- which students need extra assistance and which require a challenge
- what worked and what didn't work for motivation: Review? Application? Involvement?

## Closing a Lesson

This is the point where students themselves, regardless of age and/or experience, must summarize their learning in any way appropriate, and relate back to the initial lesson objectives shared by you. For example, with a primary class your objective might be stated as simply as, "We are going to learn how to put numbers together on a number line. This is called addition." Students' summaries, therefore, would be oral reaffirmation of the process of addition, together with a reason for the action.

Ending lessons with flair is as important as using beginnings to motivate. Consider listening to a great public speaker. You won't recall everything they said, but most likely you will remember the final words. Make your final words count. Your words, in addition to helping students understand the goal of the lesson, should encourage them to summarize for themselves. Use concise yet meaningful phrases like these:

**How-to-Wow the Perfect Lesson**
- **start with a bang**
- **use TRAIN for delivery**
- **end with a smart conclusion, new idea, or partial summary**
- **have students summarize on their own**

- *What have we been doing? Finish this sentence with your partner. "We have been busy doing/learning/sharing/trying/practicing… in order to…"*
- *I have loved doing/learning/sharing/trying/practicing _____ with you because…. Write a good sentence (of draw a picture) that tells what we have been doing.*
- *Wow! Look how much we did/learned about…. How do you think this will help us with/in/when…?*
- *Close your eyes and make a mind picture of what we just did/learned about…. Share your mind picture with the class/your neighbor/an imaginary friend.*
- *This has been exciting, doing/learning… because…. Finish the thought and share.*
- *Let's raise hands first, then call out words that let me know what we just did/learned.*

At higher levels, although you may still need to provide a quick oral summary, you should expect students to formulate more exact and substantial summaries, for themselves and to illustrate these conclusive accounts in various forms. It is better if students draw their own conclusions, as research has shown that the act of summarizing by a teacher tends to shut down a student's thinking process. It is possible to end a lesson with an interesting bit of new information; however it is still necessary for students to formulate, in their own minds, a viable summary of the lesson. Some examples of summarizing instructions:

- Write a conclusion based on what you just learned.
- Write three questions you still have related to…
- Illustrate the procedure.
- Quietly discuss the main idea of this lesson with a partner.
- Write a possible exam question based on what we just did/learned.

Basically, the closing is similar to the involvement process, but is more of a final step. It is specifically tied to the original lesson objective(s). It is a last word about the lesson—a connection of past and present with a look to where the ideas/information/skills/attitudes will take students in the future.

# The Wow of Teachable Moments and Occasions

"No matter how many plans you make or how much in control you are, life is always winging it."
— Carroll Bryant
This quote speaks directly to the teachable moments in your day. They are going to crop up no matter what you are doing, and it is in the best interest of all to make the most of them.

Teachable moments are perfect examples of the wow in teaching; they breathe new life into a classroom and leave behind memorable impressions. Capitalizing on these precious moments creates the blueprint for instilling the wow factor—excitement and electricity—into daily instruction.

You know what the teachable moment is: a spontaneous situation, unplanned-for and unpredictable, in which the class is open to new learning entirely because of something that has just happened. It can be a fleeting moment or a very valuable learning experience—it all depends on you! You can even set the stage to create teachable moments (see page 22) and then capitalize on students' natural curiosities and eagerness. Using teachable moments is way to "embrace the chaos" and forge ahead with valuable insights and information. It can be a brief flash of offered insight, or can lead into a more detailed lesson, or even unit, to follow.

Sometimes when a teachable moment occurs, the first instinct is to ignore it and continue with a pre-planned lesson. The fact that it interrupts the natural flow of the lesson can be disconcerting, until we realize just how important this chance to educate really is. Compare this to the light bulb over the head, the moment of sudden understanding or revelation, that we have all experienced. How did it feel at the time? That's the way students feel when a teachable moment occurs. The proverb "When the student is ready the teacher will appear" truly speaks to this situation, and you, the teacher, cannot afford to overlook its potential. If, however, the moment truly does interrupt something that cannot be interrupted or concentration that cannot be broken (e.g., a science experiment, a role-play activity, when on a field trip) simply acknowledge the incident, record it (in memory, on memo pad on computer or desk) and let students know you will come back to it. Just be sure you do, in fact, come back to it at a more convenient time. You will already have, or will develop, the ability to instantly be aware of a teachable moment when it arrives. It is like a tiny seed: left alone it will shrivel and die; planted and watered it can grow into something amazing. The teachable moment ignored dies; cultivated it grows. Being the conscientious educator that you are, you will cultivate these precious minutes. A way to value teachable moments is to accept the role of teacher as facilitator, as opposed to teacher as subject specialist. You do not know everything, so be prepared to admit that and seek answers and solutions with your students. In the words of a great teacher, "My job is not to answer your questions, but rather to help you find questions that are worth your time." Teachable moments may well be the way to do this.

## Recognizing Teachable Moments

Although teachable moments can occur any time, and in many forms, the following list, with actual, true anecdotes, suggests the most common of these occurrences.

### Questions

When curiosity is active and a question arises it can often be completely off topic. For example, during a science study of animals a Grade 2 student asked, "Why do animals have to poop?" The quick-thinking teacher shifted gears and the class instantly learned about digestion in both animals and humans. The off-topic question became a teachable moment. At home time, the teacher overheard the parent of the curious student ask the proverbial "What did you learn at school today?" To which the student replied, "All about poop." You can imagine the parent's thoughts.

## Discord

When discord is expressed it often leads to a teachable moment. A Grade 6 student, apparently bored with learning about history, muttered, "I don't see why we have to learn about all these old dead people." The teacher stopped his lesson and opened a discussion with the sentence, "Have you ever heard the expression *History repeats itself*?" Students shrugged or were noncommittal. He went on. "Is there something this character did or didn't do that would work today? Think about our technology and how advanced it is. If they had had our technology back then, what might have happened?" He led the discussion into a rationale for studying history that had not been a part of his original plan, but suddenly all students were totally involved.

## Disagreements

When an argument is taking place, so is a teachable moment. Two Grade 1 students were arguing over use of hot water to wash hands before lunch and were overheard by a supervising volunteer. While one student thought hot water best to kill germs, the other felt it was better to freeze them with cold water. The wise volunteer suggested they both use warm water, then take the disagreement back to class and ask their teacher. The teacher happily shared research about hand washing, use of soap, and *warm* water. Teachable moment in action!

## Natural Queries

Sometimes students wonder about things we never even think of. These natural queries lead beautifully into teachable moments and real-life learning. A custodian overheard two boys discussing where the hot water came from for the school. (They had been watching the custodian hosing down an area with obviously hot water.) The custodian stopped what he was doing and capitalized on that teachable moment by whisking both students off to the boiler room to explain the existence and workings of a water heater. Following this excursion, the two students were required to explain their findings to the rest of the class.

## Origin Unknown

Some opportunities come out of nowhere. Grade 3 students were doing math problems when out of the blue a student shouted out, "My fish had babies last night and we thought it was a boy fish." Immediately another student shouted, "My grandma's dog had two babies." The teacher, shocked at first, recognized the teachable moment and used it to initiate a lively discussion about the difference between mammals and fish.

## Unusual Activity

An unaccustomed activity, such as a fire drill, an assembly, a power outage, or a school visitor can be the prompt for an excellent teaching moment. Following a power outage, Grade 6 students were wondering why it happened and what they could do to protect power. The teacher's immediate response was to inform students that they would start studying this issue the next day. The teacher created a mini-unit to that end and the students were 100% involved.

## Beautiful Mistakes

We know we learn from mistakes, but capitalizing on them for students' benefit makes some of the most effective teachable moments. The most frequent of these seem to occur in science; a botched experiment, for example, is an amazing learning incident. However, other mistakes can be utilized as well. It requires vigilance on your part to capitalize on slip-ups and blunders and make them effective, spontaneous teaching tools. A Grade 3 student, writing a story about his favorite color, accidentally wrote "*Red is fury*" when he meant "*Red is fiery.*" When the teacher pointed this out to the student, the student asked if "fury" was an actual word. This led to a teachable moment about the meaning of the word and how it was a strong emotion.

## Restlessness

Students of all ages get restless at times. Sometimes it is the soul that is restless; sometimes it is the body in need of action. It is possible to turn this situation into a teachable moment by inquiring about the reason(s) for the disquiet. The unrest can be from differing sources that can be the basis of teachable moments, as can the fidgeting itself. A Grade 2 class was particularly unsettled during a math lesson. The teacher used this as a teachable moment by stopping her lesson, inviting students to describe how they were feeling and to offer suggestions as to why. This was the beginning of a mini-unit on feelings and how to deal appropriately with them.

## Inappropriate Stereotyping

**"Stereotypes do exist but we have to walk through them." — Forest Whitaker**

Students might inadvertently say or do things that are examples of inappropriate stereotyping. These can a teacher's nightmare, but certainly they cannot be overlooked.

These are almost mandatory teachable moments that give the teacher the chance to instill better opinions and beliefs. Reading a book about a man who was a dressmaker, a young boy in Grade 1 pointed out that "only women should be sewers." What a perfect opportunity for the teacher! She opened a discussion about gender stereotyping and every student was actively involved.

## Show & Tell…Again

Show and Tell has long been a favorite teachable moment for elementary teachers. Items brought from home, usually by younger students, are naturally interesting and can invite discussion and learning. However, students of all ages can benefit from peculiar items that may accidentally appear (e.g., a bug on a window), be brought by a student (e.g., a postcard from a distant place), or be brought by the teacher (e.g., a news clipping), especially if they are visited again in a teachable moment. In other words, if a show-and-tell item is interesting and motivating, involve the class in a do-over and revisit the item the following day with a concise, engaging, additional fact about it. A junior-high student wore an interesting tartan cap to school; the teacher saw it as a teachable moment and opened discussion about the origin of the cap. It had belonged to an ancestor from England and the discussion that followed was lively and filled with insights into English culture. The following day the teacher brought a single fact to the class; she had discovered the name of the particular tartan. The students were thrilled with this tidbit of knowledge and, needless to say, the cap-wearer wore the cap in question many more times.

## Weather

When active weather occurs, quick-thinking teachers can use the moments to discuss anything from global warming to how to dress for inclement weather. A sudden snowstorm prompted a Grade 2 teacher to invite students to discuss how settlers might have handled such conditions. This tied directly to a unit on Alberta pioneers.

## When to Hold Back—and When to Jump Right In

In all of the cases just shown, it was easier for teachers to deal with the class interruptions than ignore them. However, I realize there are times when simply bringing the class back to the focus at hand is the correct way to go.

Is it okay to be aware of a teachable moment and let it slide by? Absolutely! Not every teachable moment requires your immediate attention, and some may even be best left alone. For example, out of nowhere a Grade 2 student asked his teacher why some people lived on the street, especially in winter time; he and his mom had apparently been approached by a homeless person seeking a handout the previous day. Before his teacher could respond, another student said, "My grandpa says they are just lazy bad people who should all get jobs!" Needless to say, all activity stopped at that moment. The quick-thinking teacher, realizing this was not a topic she wanted to deal with in the classroom, said, "That is a tough question. We do have homeless people here in Edmonton. But we are not going to talk about them here and now. I want you all to talk to your parents about this." The issue was sensitive, in that it involved personal feelings and biases; the teacher skillfully defused the situation and returned the students to their tasks.

So how do you decide when to utilize a teachable moment and when not to? This depends on the age of your students and the nature or the moment, but the following guidelines may prove helpful.

Capitalize on the teachable moment...

- when the issue is at the interest and understanding levels of your students
- when it is something you personally feel comfortable dealing with
- when it doesn't involve sensitive material that will be difficult to handle; e.g., biases, spiritual beliefs, gender issues
- when the subject/lesson/task in which your class is involved will not suffer from being disrupted temporarily; non-interruptable situations might include a test, science experiment, any hands-on activity

"We forget that learning is like wall climbing. We need foot- and handholds, and the right equipment to attach or we fall. Every teachable moment is a rock jutting out from that wall, and every unique and shared perspective, or disruption in an otherwise boring day, could well be the rope that keeps us from slipping." — Jason Wyatt, teacher

- when it is something you know little about yourself; come back to this later after telling the class you will find out

Of course, you can record specifics of the teachable moments not immediately dealt with and, after consideration or perhaps research, make them into mini-lessons. You are in control and, even if the students show instant interest, your understanding of the situation will allow you to make the right decision.

## Capitalizing on Teachable Moments Using SPARK

Teachable moments are the "I didn't see that coming" moments in every teacher's life, and sometimes it is difficult to stop what you are doing and change directions entirely; even the best teachers can be temporarily lost for words. SPARK summarizes the steps that allow effective use of teachable moments when they occur.

### THE MOMENT IN QUESTION

A teacher was leading a grammar lesson when a Grade 4 student asked why grammar is important when so many cultures/people use it incorrectly.

### S = Stop/Suspend

"Life is always a matter of waiting for the right moment to act."
— Paulo Coelho
This sums up the concept of the teachable moment. The teachable moment is the right moment to act! Don't miss it in your eagerness to reach your original lesson objective, which will still be there when you return to it.

Stop what you are doing and suspend it until later. Being an aware and conscientious teacher, you will notice that teachable moments as soon as they arise. Take a quick breath, let students know you are going to stop the lesson or what they were doing, and deal with the moment enthusiastically and forcefully:

- Wow! I hadn't thought of that. Let's leave our _____ for now and we'll come back to it.
- That is a good question. Let's consider it now and return to _____ later.
- Good point! Let's look further into that and put our _____ aside for now.
- I don't know. Let's find out.
- You have really thought about…

It's important to let students know that this has been a suspension of the lesson, and that you will return to the previous lesson/activity/situation at a later time, so they don't think they can simply interrupt a lesson they don't like and have it forgotten. Remain in control of the situation.

### THE MOMENT IN QUESTION

The teacher stopped writing and said, "What a great question! Which sounds better to you: *I ain't gonna go nowhere* or *I'm not going anywhere*?"

### P = Pursue/Participate

Pursue the topic with a question and encourage active student participation. At this point, students are usually very curious and interested. You have, after all, stopped a lesson in progress, so they want to understand why. Remind students what you have been doing and tell that you will come back to it, but that for a few minutes you are going to take a look at/discuss/think about something else. Concisely summarize the new situation for them. Use phrases like these:

- ____ *brought up a very interesting* ____. *What do you think?*
- *This is interesting. Let's take a moment and...*
- *I am fascinated by... and I can see you are too, so let's...*

Encourage participation with probing questions and prompts, such as

- *Tell us about...*
- *Share what you know.*
- *What else can you tell us?*
- *Discuss it with a neighbor and be ready to share.*

THE MOMENT IN QUESTION

Students readily discussed the two sentences. They were told to talk with neighbors for a few moments and think about when each sentence might be used.

## A = Ask/Answer

Ask pertinent questions and answer queries. If there are no questions from students themselves, be sure to ask a few good ones yourself. Examples include:

- *What do you think about ...?*
- *Where can we find out about...?*
- *How does this make you feel?*
- *What would you like to know about...?*

THE MOMENT IN QUESTION

The teacher asked for student input. She answered questions regarding the correct usage then asked when/where it might be better to use the correct form; e.g., job interview, school essay, etc.

## R = Remind/Revisit

It is important to remind students of the specific learning as a closure to the teachable moment, then revisit it at a later time. Closing a teachable moment is just as important as closing a regular lesson. A simple, concise summary statement from you is all that is required, unless you plan to take the teachable moment into a series of lessons to follow.

THE MOMENT IN QUESTION

The teacher said, "So we have agreed that good English is important for certain aspects of life, but it's okay to use less-appropriate English when talking with friends."

## K = Know/Keep

Once you have concluded the moment, it is important that students know you have placed importance on the learning. You can do this by telling them when/where/how the learning will be used or will affect their lives/learning/education. In addition, you need to keep a quick record of the moment by simply jotting down the relevant learning somewhere so that you will not forget to revisit it at a later time.

A few days later, the teacher had her students role play scenarios where both good and not-so-good (formal and casual) language was used. She reminded them of what they had learned previously about language use.

## Creating Teachable Occasions

Although true teachable moments are usually unplanned-for, spontaneous happenings, it is possible to plan for some of them and make them more predictable. These are not teachable moments in the truest sense of the word, but are, nonetheless, excellent teaching occasions that do not necessarily follow the preset curriculum units of study. In these cases, the occasions are usually lengthier and more planned, but are nonetheless captivating and interesting to students. What marks these teachable occasions, as opposed to regular unit/lesson plans, is that they pop up irregularly, in various forms, due to teacher quick thinking and foresight. In other words, like true teachable moments they are rather spontaneous, but are also dependent on something specific the teacher has planned for or brought to use for quick lessons.

### Board Games

Having a variety of board games in the classroom can provide instant teachable occasions. Games today are "wise"; they are frequently based on real-life experiences. Think about Monopoly, Life, Scrabble, Connect4, etc. You can interrupt or stop a game at any time and begin a great discussion based on some fact or component of the game. Use pertinent questions or prompts such as

- *How was this game like real life?* (objective: life skills)
- *What did you like/dislike about it? Why?* (objective: forming and supporting opinions)
- *Illustrate/write about/make a jingle about the main idea of the game.* (objectives: literacy development, main idea, and communication skills)
- *Pretend you are teaching the game to your partner who has never played it before. Jot down a list of the procedure and rules.* (objectives: literacy development, communication skills)
- *There is a lot of counting in this game. What other math skills did you use?* (objective: math skills)

### Quote Cards

There is an abundance of amazing, funny, true-to-life quotes available on the Internet. Invite a volunteer (and older student, parent volunteer, aide, or even spouse or offspring) to collect a variety of interesting quotes and print them on small file cards. Quotes can be funny or inspirational. Here are a few examples:

- *May the forces of evil become confused on the way to your house.* (A connection to well-known Star Wars movies)
- *Four out of three people struggle with math.*
- *The only way to get a friend is to be a friend.*
- *You're braver than you believe, stronger than you seem and smarter than you think.* (A.A. Milne)

Knowing that quotes are readily available is not enough. Now you need to know how to use them in a time-efficient manner.

1. Choose a quote card at random.
2. Either read it to the class or invite a student to read it out loud.
3. Lead a debriefing discussion and/or activity, using prompt questions:

   - What does this quote mean?
   - How does it apply to you/life/our world?
   - Illustrate the quote.
   - Write a story/essay/paragraph/sentence based on the quote.
   - Do you like/dislike this quote? Why?
   - Write another quote that has a similar meaning.

## News Items

Since news is current and constantly changing, any item clipped from a newspaper (Yes, I know these are almost things of the past, but why not introduce students to these very important recordings of history?) is relevant. A great photo is best, but with older students a short text clip works too. Share the photo/clipping/editorial and discuss. Students can locate news clips on their devices if that works for you. Of course, discussion specifically about the photo/clipping is mandatory, but can be followed by a more abstract discussion that encourages students to think more deeply.

1. Tell the class you are going to look at the news.
2. Share the chosen photo/clipping.
3. Ask probing questions, such as

   - What *is* news? (younger students)
   - How is news collected for papers/Internet?
   - How true do you think this is? Can we believe it entirely?
   - Why do reporters make what they write sound so graphic/terrible/funny/scary/etc.?
   - How do they do that?
   - Specifically what information is this trying to give us?
   - Can you identify how the writer feels about the situation? How do you know?
   - What is fake news? How can we tell if a clip is fake?
   - Write a news clip about… (some relevant in-school happening)

## Real-Life Happenings

We never know what is going to happen in life from one moment to the next, and sometimes a "happening" makes a worthy discussion starter or classroom lesson. How this differs from the traditional teachable moment is that the event doesn't happen right then and there in the classroom with students as witnesses, but rather occurs elsewhere, at a different time. You can capitalize on happenings by sharing them and guiding discussion and/or class activities. Here are a few examples:

   - Lost car keys that led to frantic searches
   - An amusing antic of a pet
   - A silly thing you did by mistake

- Something humorous (or serious) that happened to someone you know
- A burned meal (kids love to hear about adults burning toast)

"Something wonderful is about to happen, and something awful is about to happen. You can dwell on either one. It's your choice."
— Richelle E. Goodrich
You can use this quote as a quick teachable moment when sharing an amusing, but negative, anecdote, to remind students that dwelling on negative happenings is a poor choice.

If you want to create a teachable occasion from a happening, it is relatively quick and easy, and usually highly motivating.

1. Quickly share the incident or happening
2. Open discussion in such as way as to lead to your objectives. For instance, with the lost keys, a lesson on organization could easily follow, so you would want to start with a question to suggest organizational skills.
3. Use probing questions. Here are some possible opening questions:

- Has anything like this ever happened to you or to someone you know?
- What could I learn from this?
- Is there a better way to…?

4. Summarize the discussion by drawing some conclusions. Make reference to the learning you wanted to create, for example:

- Write me a letter telling me how to avoid this situation in the future.
- Role play with a peer this happening to you.

## Strange Holidays

All teachers make excellent use of holidays and special events by decorating classrooms and creating work that reflects the occasion. These are teachable occasions. But I suggest the use of less-familiar holidays as teaching tools. The Internet offers literally hundreds of these, and you can pick and choose according to your students' interests and ages. Here are just a few to give you the idea:

January 8 is National Bubble Bath Day
January 15 is National Strawberry Ice Cream Day
January 24 is National Compliment Day
January 30 (my personal favorite) is National Bubble Wrap Appreciation Day
January 31 is National Milk Day

It is fun to take a look at some of these and use them as a teachable occasion. Here are some leading questions:

- Who do you think came up with this one and why?
- How does this relate to us today?
- Make a poster advertising this special day.
- What is one thing you might do to celebrate this day?
- Create your own special day and write a slogan for it.

## Following Up

When I talk about follow-up, I am referring to additional lessons and/or activities prompted by the teachable moment but pursued at a later date. Of course, not all true teachable moments require follow-up. Often you will simply reinforce learning from a moment with a statement such as, "Remember what we talked about yesterday when…" However, should you want to develop the learning further, here are some how-to suggestions. It is best to wait a day or two before revisiting the moment and, when you do, do so with the enthusiasm that originally accompanied the teachable moment minilesson. Re-investigating or restudying a teachable moment is one of the wise teacher's most motivating strategies. Any of these activities can bring that teachable moment back to life.

### Role Play the Moment

Remind students of the teachable moment and invite them to act it out where possible. This role play is specific to the teachable moment and can include speech, gestures, or even mime. For example, a few days following a fire drill and the accompanying teaching of fire safety, students in small groups could act out the rules of fire safety in mime form, while the rest of the class tries to identify the rule(s). If the teachable moment was based on an item brought to the class, students role play with a partner the use or function of the item.

### Interviewing

This activity divides students into interviewers and interviewees, and invites them to ask questions of each other related to the teachable moment from a previous day. Students of all ages enjoy this activity and, after a few prompting questions from you, can really become involved. The following example comes from a Grade 4 classroom: A student had brought an authentic-looking tomahawk to school, explaining it had belonged to his great-grandfather and his father finally allowed him to share it. You can imagine how much was learned about Indigenous peoples. The following day the students took part in interviewing each other about the tomahawk.

Boy 1: What is that interesting thing called?
Boy 2: A tomahawk. It's really old.
Boy 1: Can you tell me something about it?
Boy 2: It's made of stone and wood, and the handle is wrapped with cord. Probably the cord was colored but the color has worn off.
Boy 1: What was it used for?
…

### Diorama

Depending on the learning, inviting students in an art class to create a diorama about it can be very effective. For example, following the learning about various strange special holidays, they could choose one (e.g., National Milk Day) and create a scene depicting what people might do to celebrate this day.

### Scripting

Older students can be asked to write a short script that requires the characters to provide information about the learning in an interesting or funny way. The script should be of the readers theatre variety, to be shared as round-table reading rather than actually be acted out. For example, following a period of extreme weather that forced the shut-down of school for two days, a teacher involved students in a teachable moment about global warming. The next day they wrote scripts related to what they had learned; here is a short excerpt:

Mr. Old Man: I am so cold. When I was a kid it was never like this. We had winter, sure, but this is crazy.

Young Boy: It's because of global warming.

Mr. Old Man: Global warming! Never heard of it.

Young Girl: Our atmosphere has turned into a blanket because of the carbon dioxide gas. We have too many cars and stuff.

Mr. Old Man: Nonsense!

Young Boy: It's true. We have to cut down on pollution.

…

## Creating Word Puzzles

Have students brainstorm words associated with the teachable moment, then create crossword puzzles, word searches, or scrambled-word puzzles for peers to solve. This activity not only reinforces what was learned, but also provides practice in vocabulary and spelling.

# Chapter 2 Teaching the Curriculum

Teachers are always right, right? Wrong! It would be impossible to learn and retain all the curricular content teachers are expected to deliver. What teacher are masters at, however, is knowing how and where to find information, and being skilled at digging into that huge manuscript called curriculum and creating ways to effectively deliver it to students. I don't think anyone ever covers every single bit of a curriculum. Curricula are massive manuscripts with lots of room for teacher preferences, but the basic framework of them, the tenets on which they have been built, must be the basis of your units and lessons. It is your professional responsibility to follow the established curriculum. How you do that is usually left up to you, but you must always have it in the back of your mind when planning lessons and units.

1. Before the year begins, take time to familiarize yourself with the curriculum, even if is the same one you've taught for years. You don't have to read it in detail—skim and highlight. The idea is to develop an awareness of what the curriculum includes and what the specific goal objectives are.
2. Depending on the format of your curriculum, it can be a good idea to photocopy sections and have loose sheets on your desk you can use like a checklist to mark completed portions.
3. Using pencil (so it can be erased later) write the dates beside finished sections of the curriculum. This helps you see at a glance exactly where you are.
4. At natural school breaks, like Christmas and spring break, take a bit of time to once again scan the curriculum, paying attention to areas not yet covered. Future plans should focus on covering these areas.
5. Some teachers develop a personal code for connecting specific lessons/units directly to the curriculum. For instance, *SS1.3* written beside a social studies lesson could indicate that the goals from the curriculum that were being covered by that lesson were in Social Studies part 1, section 3. This might seem a bit time-consuming but it certainly keeps you connected to curriculum.

*What* you teach will depend primarily on the curricula for established for your area. *How* you teach it is up to you. From content instruction, through helping your students develop and train their memories, to teaching spelling and grammar in their social-media driven world, you want to use methods that will engage students and make your job as easy as possible. The how will change and develop with practice, but this chapter includes some ideas to help you initially, or give you a boost if you are already experienced.

# Content Instruction

Content refers to the body of facts and knowledge you have to provide for students. The most common method of delivery of content is the lecture method. Think back to a time when you were a lecture recipient—at university, teachers' professional day(s), in a meeting or church, for example. What sparked your interest? Or lack of interest? Did the speaker keep your attention or did your mind wander?

How can you be an attention-keeper when you have to impart facts to your class? The creation of a little wow in content instruction usually comes from using cues familiar to the students, from tying content to what they already know and what they need or want to know. Impress them with preparation, experience, knowledge, and expertise about the content, or, alternatively, with your enthusiastic desire to pursue with the students what you do not know. You want to wow them with your wit and awareness of their needs.

The lecture method can be effective if used appropriately, either as a brief minilecture, or as a concentrated, very focused discourse on a topic (usually for older students). However, there are other great ways to help students gain an awareness of, understand, and process content. In fact, as a good teacher, you will be using a variety of these methods of conveying content every day.

## Adding Wow to Lectures

### Start with a Handout or Chart

Providing students with an outline, either in the form of a handout or as a clearly visible chart, is a viable tool for increasing the effectiveness of a lecture-format lesson. This guides their thinking, cues them to important points, and lets them know the objective(s) of the talk. The handout can be an outline or in Q&A form. In the latter, concise questions lead students toward finding answers in the content of your talk. Answers should be short—even single words—so as not to take students' attention from the rest of the lesson.

### Tie in to Student Interest and Desire

Know your students and start by letting them know how the information you are going to share is important, or has meaning for them. Tie the learning to what they already know, and to what they might need in their lives. Tell them what the personal benefits will be. For example, before a history lesson, point out how history has affected them today. Before a math lesson, remind them that they will require these skills to understand their salaries later in life (or their allowances now), or perhaps to someday acquire a job in technology.

### Start with a Mysterious Question

Start with a question that is both thought-provoking and a bit mysterious. For example, before a lesson on ecosystems, ask, "What would happen if pollution got so bad we were overrun with garbage everywhere?" or "Who has seen the Disney movie WALL-E?" or "If you turned on your tap and there was no water, what would you do?" The question will lead to your lesson objective. Be creative.

The task is to catch attention, not spend a lot of time answering the question. Older students who have been introduced to the idea of a rhetorical question will quickly learn to eagerly anticipate your rhetorical questions.

### Do the Unexpected

If you usually stand at the front of your class, move to a different part of the room and speak from there. Just this simple change will capture attention. Another change might include donning a hat or piece of clothing; I watched a teacher put on a single glove before talking about the industrial revolution and the consequent use of factories for retail production. Or you might turn off the lights and deliver in the dark, or use a pointer or stick to tap on your desk at pertinent points during your lecture.

### Mix It Up

Mix facts with common-sense details and questions as much as possible. *Talk less, discuss more*, is a good rule to follow. Mix in visuals, music, tactile elements—anything that will keep students constantly alert. Rely on the familiar theory of intermittent reinforcement by quizzing and praising students for listening at random points. Questions like these work well:

- What four words stood out in what I just told you?
- Think of one sentence that summarizes the facts so far and share with a neighbor.
- In your notes, jot down any words or thoughts you have so far.
- Write a good test question based on what I have just told you.
- I am going to give true/false statements about the information just shared. Put thumbs up to indicate *true* and thumbs down to indicate *false*.

Students love this last one. It is a unthreatening way to reinforce concepts and assess what has been learned.

### Be Authentic and Captivating

Think back again to a lecturer who caught and held your attention. Most probably their voice changed frequently and their body language morphed regularly. So, to follow suit, be enthusiastic. Talk quickly, then slowly. Talk loudly, then softly. Inject a bit of an accent here and there if you can. Give a few details in chant, sing-song, or rap. Move around the room. Lean, turn your back, cross your arms, sit on your desk, lift your hands high, snap your fingers, open your palms out. Keep moving!

## Other Approaches

Content delivery does not have to be boring. How you deliver it makes a world of difference to how students hear and accept it, and consequently makes your job easier. Giving a monologue to students is not the only way to impart facts. Approaches are limited only by your own imagination.

## Use Technology

Have students do online research after you have provided key prompts, questions, or cues. (Avoid random web surfing.) Then have them share their findings, acting as the teachers of their peers.

## Project Approach

In order to complete a project, students need to research content and show mastery over that content. Students are actively involved in their own learning. Usually projects are used alongside other teaching strategies and approaches; the projects complement the other methodologies. The project approach entails selection of topic, collection of data, presentation and culmination of project.

1. Introduce a topic of study related to your curriculum and objectives.
2. Discuss the topic and break it into manageable project goals. In other words, if the curriculum goal is *study of community*, help students break this into manageable components, such as service jobs, retail, wholesale; or the baker, the meat shop, the beauty parlor, etc.
3. Assign specific projects to individuals or pairs, taking personal interest into account. One experienced teacher had most of her students wanting to do projects on the same topic. No problem. Rather than trying to force students into areas of less interest, she allowed several similar projects, then used them for a comparative analysis at the end.
4. Allow class time for projects, but encourage at-home involvement too.
5. Set a due date and stick to it.
6. Be alert to chances (teachable moments) to teach skills from other areas (e.g., math, literacy) during the development of the projects.

## Gaming

There are many online educational games available. Your job is to select the one(s) that promote content learning in the areas of your curriculum. The new educational version of Minecraft is a good example. Students do not need encouragement to play these games, and they learn content while honing tech skills. Just be sure to identify your goal or objective and share it with students. In other words, tell them what you expect them to learn.

## Virtual Field Trip

You appreciate the value of field trips, but are also are aware of their cost in dollars, as well as time and energy. So why not take a virtual field trip? A virtual field trip combines the best of technology with the natural curiosity of students, and no one ever has to leave the classroom. Follow the formula for computer research: research; gather and compile data; prepare and present.

1. Define clearly, for yourself and for students, the objective of the virtual field trip. There may be several objectives. List them concisely and discuss in class.
2. You will have already formed a list of available resources (museums, art galleries, public speakers, other classrooms around the world, etc.). Select the resources you want your students to use and make them visually apparent on charts, posters, hand-outs, etc.

3. Discuss with students how to take a virtual field trip.
4. Discuss time management. Tell students how long they will have to gather data, compile information, prepare final projects.
5. Let them go to work. Stick to time schedules. This encourages consistent work in whatever area students are in.

## Incomplete Content

This is a content-retrieval strategy in which students are provided with partial information and encouraged to complete the content through whatever means you, or they, choose. Resources might include text books, library resources, Internet sites. The idea is to stimulate interest by sharing part of the subject, theme, or problem, and having students seek the missing components. The appeal is like reading or watching a cliff-hanger. Not all content material is conducive to this approach, but when it is, it can be very effective.

1. Share the basic lesson content objective(s) For example, "We are going to learn about how frogs help the environment. They are extremely important to us for many reasons, and they are disappearing at a rapid rate. There are specific reasons for this."
2. Add a touch of mystery or interest. For example, "I am going to tell you about their sensitive skin, then you are going to find out how and why they are disappearing."
3. Send students off to find locate the missing information, record it, and bring it back to class.
4. Share the findings so that content has been covered completely.

## Teacher's Sick Day

Teachers, like parents, are not allowed sick days. You put on your teacher face and work no matter how you are feeling. You are a consummate actor and you play your part, but once in a while, fake it! Tell students you need a teacher's sick day, and you want them to teach each other. Once you get them involved, circulate and enjoy your sick day.

1. Specifically write the lesson objective in the form of a descriptive sentence that delineates exactly what content the lesson should involve. For example, "In math today we need to focus on the meaning of the word *variables* in algebra, as opposed to the term *arbitrary number*. Then we need to understand how arithmetic and algebra are both the same and different. There are two concepts here."

**Aristotle said that in order to teach you must first understand. Students teaching students is a perfect demonstration of this truth.**

2. Divide the class into pairs. Each partner assumes responsibility for researching and teaching one concept to the other partner.
3. Discuss where students will look for the content, how they will remember and/or record it, and how they will teach it.
4. Follow specific time constraints, depending on the amount of content to be covered.
5. Students are usually very good at this so there is no need for debriefing, but you can check by using brief quiz questions or a whole-class Q&A.

# Training and Encouraging Memory

Memory is the personal journal you carry with you everywhere you go. Since you cannot erase it or leave it behind, you might as well try to keep it sharp and useful.

Recall a failed attempt to remember a name, where you put your keys, what time an appointment was scheduled for. When you do remember, what you feel is a perfect example of wow. Think of the excited feeling, the rush, that accompanied that wow. This is what you help students experience by assisting them with memory enhancement. Students get excited when they work on memory development. They are thrilled when they can remember important facts, skills, and concepts. They are encountering an impressive wow factor, and you will be sharing it with them.

## Memory Basics

There are two forms of memory. The first is short-term, sometimes called working memory, which consists of encoding, storage, and retrieval. The second is long-term memory, responsible for storage of information over long periods of time. In the classroom, you are mostly concerned with short-term memory and its three components.

Despite the convenience and easy accessibility of information on the Internet, students today have more to remember than ever before; I don't think anyone would argue this point. And many of them struggle with short-term memory, which makes teaching even more difficult. There are memory basics you can teach to help your students develop and enhance their memories.

- Discuss memory in class. Talk about how it helps us, and how we actually can improve its functioning. Drawing memory to students' attention when you begin helps them focus on memory-related tasks thereafter. This is called priming the memory and is a useful strategy in all teaching.
- Plan specific minilessons that stimulate memory. (See page 33.)
- Remind students when they need to turn on their memories specifically. For example, before memorizing mathematical facts like multiplication tables, say "Turn on the memories. Think and remember."
- Use memory priming tasks at lesson onset, or whenever you specifically want students to remember. This is especially important when giving directions. Some students will remember the last direction but forget how to get started.

## Giving Directions

By following the process outlined here, you can help students to be ready to remember when directions are given. They quickly become an integral part of every good teacher's repertoire.

### GET ATTENTION

If students are not totally tuned in to you, giving directions can be both useless and frustrating. In order to stimulate short-term memory so they can encode, store, and quickly retrieve all the directions in the correct order, they first need to give you their full attention. Use whatever tricks you can to get this.

Give directions verbally and visually. Students should be able to hear and see the directions.

### CHECK UNDERSTANDING

Immediately check for understanding by asking several students to repeat the directions back to you. If the directions are still a bit unclear, or if you are not convinced of their complete understanding, ask a student to explain the directions for the class.

### USE EXAMPLES

It may seem superfluous to say, but sharing just a couple of examples of what you expect can make the world of difference, especially for students struggling with short-term memory. They see the finished product; that can stimulate memories.

## Memory Enhancement Techniques

The techniques and tips shared here may not be new to you, but some of the how-to suggestions for incorporating them in your teaching may be. In any event, every teacher needs reminding occasionally. Our memories, too, always need honing and enhancing. Let's teach students how to improve their memories. There are several tricks and techniques that seem to work well with students of all ages. Remember to let them know that these are for memory improvement. Drawing memory to their minds frequently serves to increase awareness of the importance of focusing and remembering when important content is being shared.

### Skim It First

Teach students to first take a quick look at any page of content they are hoping to store in memory, even if it is a page of basic math facts. They must get a general idea in their minds of what is to come. Looking at titles, headings, footnotes, etc. helps the brain prepare to remember.

### Learn and Learn and Learn Again

The name of this technique refers to the idea of overlearning a concept or piece of knowledge. Most of us learn by repeating a few times, then assuming the tidbit of information has moved into long-term memory. Good on you, if this is the case for you. What works best for most of us, and certainly for students, is learning and learning again. Learning occurs only if knowledge is in long-term memory. One way to see if this has happened is to test students on a learning several weeks after sharing it with them. If they know it as well as they should, continue on. If they are stumbling, then they have to relearn. The trick is to make the relearning interesting for them, not like boring repetition.

1. Introduce the strategy of overlearning. Explain that this will help students remember not only school facts, but also whatever they need to remember in the rest of their lives.

2. Share a concept, math fact, lines of poetry, etc., and together repeat it several times.
3. Stop. Pause. Repeat it again. Do the stop/pause several more times.
4. Move on to another task, then come back to the memorization and repeat again.
5. Check the learning several weeks later.
6. If relearning is required, find a different motivating opening and/or different tasks to assess the learning. Avoid exact repetition of the original learning.

## Chunking

In this technique, things or words or pieces of content are grouped together so they can be remembered as a single concept. Chunking makes information easier to retain and recall, and is a skill that can be taught to students. The most familiar form of chunking is in the recall of phone numbers. We automatically combine individual numbers into larger chunks for easier recall. Some students may chunk automatically, but this skill usually isn't in place until late elementary. However, a Grade 1 student was overheard saying about a list of spelling words, "I'm going to chunk this stuff so I can remember it." The other students were curious, as was the teacher, who asked the student to explain. Unfortunately, this student's idea of chunking was to break the words down, rather than to put content together. It was a perfect teachable moment for the wise teacher. We can, and should, teach students to chunk.

1. Explain what chunking is, in terms students can understand. Students like the word, and once they gain confidence with the technique, will use it freely and correctly.
2. Talk about connections. How do items fit together? Do they start with the same letter? Do they share a purpose?
3. Practice chunking, starting with simple lists. Start with a spelling or vocabulary list and discuss how to group the words. For example, all 4-letter words, all words with silent *e*, all words that relate to a topic.
4. Talk about association (although you may not want to use that term with younger students). Point out how, if several items can be associated (related or connected) to something else, it will be easier to remember them. For example, when trying to remember a series of steps in a science experiment, if the steps can be compared to steps in some other activity (baking, playing soccer) they will be easier to remember.
5. Practice together and individually, and often. When an occasion arises that could call for chunking, point it out and reinforce the technique.

## Use the Mind's Eye

This is the strategy of attaching a mind image to something to be memorized. As adults we often do this unconsciously, but students need to be taught the technique.

1. Start with funny or unusual names that lend themselves to colorful images. For example, Bella Livingston might be remembered as "a bell made of stone."
2. Do some name images together, sharing the alternative method of visualizing a person's name by connecting it to how they look. For example, a very tall man called Jack Upstead, could be associated with Jack and the Beanstalk (tall

giant), and how Jack climbed up (*Up*stead) the beanstalk. Not all names will work as easily as these, but students become quite efficient at creating visual images for names once they understand the technique.

3. Broaden this idea to concepts other than names. Ask students how they can see the concept in their minds. In this way, the memorized content becomes the cue for a visualization, which in turn helps students remember details.

### Make It Memorable

In this technique, whatever is being read to remember, such as pages of important text, are marked up in such a way as to make it visually eye-catching and dynamic. We have all used highlighters—often to an extreme where it becomes meaningless. You can teach students of all ages how to use this technique wisely, as a tool to promote memory. In fact, it has been demonstrated that the mere act of making it memorable improves memory, even if the spotlighted text is never again reviewed.

1. Discuss the importance of identifying the most salient points in a text and making them stand out to help with memorization.
2. Together practice identifying key or main points in a selection. Point out the danger of overhighlighting and discuss the idea that "less is more." Practicing the skill of identifying important content is a necessary step in developing better memory skills. We need to remember only the important material. More than that is impossible and confusing.
3. Discuss various ways to make sections or words memorable. For example:
   - different colors of highlighter organized according to importance
   - notes or sketches in margins
   - circling, starring, or boxing key words/phrases
   - keeping a jot pad handy and jotting down key points/words at the end of a page or section. This mental connection works well for many students.

### Mnemonics

"Without memory there is no culture. Without memory there would be no civilization, no society, no future. " — Elie Wiesel

Discuss and develop cues or mnemonics for memory enhancement. For example, to remember the Great Lakes, students use the acronym HOMES (Huron, Ontario, Michigan, Erie, Superior). Once students are familiar with this technique they quickly create their own cues to help recall content of any kind.

## Memory-Enhancing Games

The following games are fun and effective and can be used in the middle of other tasks as motivational techniques or ways to take a break.

### Card Games

There are many simple card games that encourage remembering. In one easy game, a deck of cards is turned face-down and students in small groups (of about four) take turns turning them over to find matches. Other simple games like Go Fish encourage younger students to remember what cards other players hold. More complicated games, such as Whist or even Bridge, encourage older students to focus and remember what cards have been played.

1. Introduce a card game period (about 10 minutes) as a way to improve memory.
2. Discuss an age-dependent choice of games.
3. Be sure to have enough decks of cards.
4. Allow free play, but watch the time restraints. Remind students when time is almost up.
5. Debrief quickly by asking how the game(s) might stimulate memory. Awareness is the key ingredient in success.

## Add-Ons

This effective memory game can take several forms, but basically it involves students adding words or phrases to a beginning cue, and at the same time recalling all that has been said previously. This can take a storytelling format in which an actual story is built by constantly adding to the beginning, for example:

Cue: The boy...
2. The boy ran...
3. The boy ran away...
4. The frightened boy ran away...

Alternatively, the add-ons can create simply a list of words:

Cue: cat
2. cat, rat
3. cat, rat, food
4. cat, rat, food, see

Random words can take whatever form you want, either totally random (as in the example) or following a theme, such as "must rhyme" or "must be related to science study of..." You can introduce a fun element by passing a small ball or beanbag around; whoever has the ball must add the next word/phrase while recalling all that has been said previously. If they get it correct, they throw the ball to someone else; if they get it incorrect, they are out.

1. Introduce Add-Ons as a memory improving game.
2. Explain whatever guidelines you have decided on; e.g., theme.
3. Break the class into teams (optional but fun). If a team player cannot come up with a word in three seconds, or forgets what has been said previously, the other teams get a point.
4. Debrief by discussing how the game improves memory.

## Concentration/Match Up

Like the games described as card games (page 35), this game involves matching of any similar or same items or pairs. There are many commercial decks available, but it is possible to have students make their own. Each student designs two index cards in the same manner. When cards are placed face down and shuffled, students try to locate pairs. The student with the most pairs at the end of the game wins.

### Coding for Memory

In keeping with technology, this simple memory enhancement game uses coding for players to move in various directions, both stimulating memory and reinforcing technology skills. You will need graph paper for the game or, for younger students, copied sheets with lines.

1. Introduce a path-creating game in which students compare their paths to a master path.
2. If you haven't done anything with coding, explain how to move in various directions from a starting point to create a line that moves across the page.
3. Model by plotting a few moves on your master.
4. To stimulate memory, you can give one cue at a time (e.g., 3R = move 3 spaces to the right) or several cues at once (3R, 2D, 4L).
5. Plan the route ahead of time so that, once you have given all the cues and students have created their paths, they can compare with the master.
6. Repeat the activity as many times as you wish, making memory more and more important as you go by giving more cues at a time. Caution: Remember the steps for giving good directions (see page 32).
7. Debrief by discussing how playing this game helps with memory, what was easy/hard about it, and how students might improve the technique for the next time.

### Poetry and Script

**What kids know by rote is not as important as their ability to think and understand. However, memorization of some basic facts and content is what allows students to move ahead with their education.**

Memorization of lines of poetry and/or simple script is an excellent way to enhance memory. If you use this technique, be sure to present the memorized material, otherwise students won't see the value in what they are doing. Humorous poems are often the most interesting to younger children. For longer poems, have several students work together, breaking the poem into manageable chunks for memorization.

### Online Memory Games

There are so many online memory games that it is a matter of teacher choice which ones to use in class or to suggest to parents as good learning tools. A particularly good site is National Geographic Kids (https://kids.nationalgeographic.com/explore/adventure_pass/memory-games) but there are many others. Students want to use technology. Encourage them to use it to enhance memory. Brain games stimulate and help improve memory, but only if used sparingly and within the daily screen time for students (Most studies recommend no more than two hours a day).

### Directions Pyramid

In this game, students are given directions in a continually more difficult manner, making it necessary for them to remember all the previous directions as well as the most current one. The first direction becomes the base of the pyramid; it governs the rest of the directions. For example, here are some examples of first directions:

- Stand up beside your desk.
- Take out a blank sheet of paper.
- Go to a spot in the room where you can have an imaginary bubble around you.
- Place your math book on your desk.

You can see how any of these first directions leads the way for what is to follow. And what follows is a series of directions that must all be remembered and followed in correct sequence until the final direction, the point of the pyramid (the point of the exercise), is reached. This sounds more complicated than it is. Some students will retrieve all the directions, while others will borrow ideas from peers. Either way, you have incorporated a quick memory enhancer into a daily classroom event.

1. Discuss the pyramid shape and how the base holds everything else.
2. Provide your base direction and allow students to follow it immediately.
3. Provide several more directions in order, pausing for about 5 seconds after each. Older students are not allowed to talk or write, but they can be reminded of memory tricks, such as saying it over to yourself in your mind. With younger students, it is okay and helpful for them to practice verbal rehearsal by repeating the directions out loud in any way they want to. (Some children use a sing-song voice. Some repeat only the most recent direction. Some go back to the beginning and repeat from there each time; this is the most effective way.)
4. Choose your directions so that the final direction is obviously the pyramid peak or final step in the exercise.

Some examples will clarify:

Physical Movement Pyramid Directions
1. Stand by your desk.
2. Raise your arms to the sides.
3. Put one foot on your seat.
4. Tap the toe on the seat.
5. Open your mouth.
6. Sing "aahhhhhhhhhhhh."

Math (Core Subject) Direction Pyramid
1. Take out your math book.
2. Open to page 34.
3. Skim the page.
4. Mark only the questions that start with the word *The*.
5. Do every other one of these questions, starting with number 5.
6. Close your book.
7. Put your hands together on your desk.

## Suitcase Game

While I'm sure this is familiar to you, I have included it here for its wonderful, instant memory-enhancing benefits. Children take turns saying what they will add to a suitcase, each time repeating all that has gone before. Or they add items, avoiding (through memory) what has already been added. The former is more difficult. In both cases, when a student falters, forgets, or repeats an item, they are out. If you veer away from elimination games, you can play it as a points-earned game in which every correct response earns a point either for a team or an individual.

## A Backward Step

Simply having students think backward on any simple task promotes memory encoding and retrieval, and is an important skill to have for lifelong learning.

1. At completion of a task (story, math problem, science experiment, larger project, art project, etc.), have students stop and think about what they have just done. Allow about 2 minutes of silence for thinking.
2. Have students start at the ending of the task (story conclusion, answer to math problem, outcome of science experiment, etc.) and think backward.
3. With young students, review backward steps orally. Have older students jot down points that indicate the steps in backward progression.
4. Debrief by pointing out how sometimes we need to look back to find errors or faults.

## Routines and Choreography

**"We should consider every day lost in which we have not danced at least once." — Friedrich Nietzsche**

Dancers and stage fighters have long sequences of actions to remember, and a single mistake can be disastrous. And dancing is one of the most basic forms of expression. You can capitalize on this idea in the classroom by teaching students a simple dance routine or series of choreographed fight steps.

You don't have to be a dancer to do this. There are literally hundreds of videos on YouTube demonstrating simple steps that are easy to follow. Students really enjoy this, even if they complain initially. Make it even more fun by adding a favorite tune. Here is a simple sample combination of dance moves that, when put together, make for a fun presentation and a great memory enhancer.

**A great idea is to have students create and teach their peers other routines. Look at all the memory!**

1. March and clap 8 times.
2. March 4 steps, lifting knee on the fourth count. Repeat 4 times
3. Step legs apart, turn to the side, and bounce 4 times to each side while rolling arms in front.
4. Turn back to the front and do grapevine move (4 steps to the side with a tap on fourth step to allow direction change) 2 times in each direction.

## On the Tray

This is another familiar memory game that often serves as a party game. Place as many items as possible on a tray, have students observe it for 60 seconds, then cover it and have them try to recall as many items as possible. This can be a team game with the team getting the most items winning. Or it can be an individual game. This is an excellent prelude to teaching or reinforcing the chunking strategy as, after a first try, the class can chunk the items together and try again. It's quite remarkable to see the improvement chunking makes.

# Spelling and Grammar in a World of Social Media

It is certainly true that social media has taken over the world, so teachers must know how to deal effectively with its influence on students. Philosophical questions like "Does social media affect perception of reality?" or "Does social media affect thinking and perception of self?" are beyond the scope of this book. But, in the context of linguistics, it will share a few ideas for helping students appreciate and deal with the differences between communication on social media and in school-related tasks.

Although most parents make a constituted effort to restrict or limit their children's use of social media, it is still an issue. Children are easily manipulated and swayed. But social media can be a useful tool for students to use to make connections that can help them with careers and life in general. With that in mind, you can make it a point to use social media in your classroom in positive ways.

The expression, *If you can't beat 'em, join 'em*, applies here. Social media is here to stay, so let's make it work for us in the classroom. There is so much available online to assist you with this, I will only touch briefly on the topic.

- Help students see the values of social media as a source of information by following one of your main unit objectives on Twitter or by blogs about the topic.
- Have students set up a blog and post writing assignments for others to read and comment on. When you teach them how to comment productively, you are teaching them good editing skills for their own work.
- Check out sites like Scoop, Tumblr, and Pinterest to see if they can work for you. If you are not comfortable with a site, don't use it. Your complete contentment with the site is mandatory.

## Spelling

"Even though being a good speller has lost its ranking in school, we can hope there is one group of artisans that still finds spelling important—the tattoo artist."
— Nanette L. Avery

Perhaps the area where technology has played the most havoc with linguistics is spelling, with grammar coming a close second. It has been said that poor spelling instruction is a national epidemic. But is spelling it important? When everyone texts "r u cmg" for "are you coming," is there really a need for good spelling? The answer is yes. Absolutely. Because only by mastering the basics of spelling until it is automatic can students move toward the higher-order thinking and good communication skills necessary for success in careers and life in general. And research tells us that proficient spelling improves reading fluency and comprehension—skills absolutely mandatory for life.

So what, then, can you do to improve the spelling skills of students, no matter what their age? Obviously the younger the student, the more important this is, but poor spelling reaches all the way through middle school to high school, and even (I speak from first-hand experience) into post-secondary studies. Take away spellcheck and suddenly the majority of students is lost. If, in fact, spelling is closely associated with reading competency, then it behooves us to take a critical look at how we are handling spelling in the classroom. Once again, there is a plethora of help online for the actual teaching of spelling. But here are a few extras, games, and tricks of which you may not be aware.

First, allow me to remind you that teaching spelling in context is simply the best approach.

- If you want to use spelling lists, use the words in sentences.
- Constantly point out spelling words in content text, narratives, posters, online text, signs, etc.
- When giving spelling quizzes, have students write entire short sentences with the spelling words in them. You can mark only the specific words, but having those words immersed in sentences makes the process much more meaningful.

## Spelling Games

See page 81 for more spelling games.

While not necessarily games in the sense of competitions or contests, these activities are fun for students, and keep them moving toward being better spellers without even being aware of it.

### CLOAKED CROSSWORDS

Cloaked crosswords are vertical and horizontal letter boxes overlapping and connected as a crossword puzzle would be, but missing the clues of regular crossword puzzles, hence *cloaked*. The number of boxes per row, as well as the number of rows, can be varied according to students' ages and abilities. Usually I start with one row made up of a longer word in the middle horizontally, with various other rows of boxes springing from it. Since there are no clues, there are no right or wrong answers, and students attempt to fill in all the rows with any words that fit together.

### BIG WORD, LITTLE WORD

**This is a great pairs game; the pair with the most little words wins.**

Provide students with a long compound word from their spelling and/or core vocabulary. In a given time limit, students make as many small words as possible from the letters in the big word. For example,

Big Word: *arithmetic*
Little Words: *met, the, rat cat*, etc.

You can make a variation of the game by allowing one "free letter." Students can choose any letter to add to the letters in the big word to allow them to create more little words. This taps beautifully into spelling memory, as the letter they choose should be capable of being used many times. For example, if students chose to add an *s* to the big word *arithmetic*, the plural forms of most of the little words can be made. You can make the game more difficult by limiting the extra letter to vowels, a silent *e*, or the spelling concept you want to reinforce.

### BOARD GAMES

Many board games available today involve and reinforce spelling, with Scrabble being one of the most familiar. Keep a few of these available in your classroom for supplementary activities and spelling reinforcement. A few good ones are Scrabble, Spelligator, Bananagrams, and Chunks.

### ONLINE GAMES

Like board games, online games do an amazing job of reinforcing spelling and are highly motivating for students. There are literally hundreds of sites from which to choose, but a few excellent online spelling games include School Bus Spelling,

Short i Vowel Games, Short Vowel Cat Food games, and Common Noun Mud Hop. Use games such as these freely to bolster and support spelling.

### FRIENDED VOWELS

Based on the social media concept of *friending*, this game requires students to locate, in a paragraph or selected piece of text, all the vowels who have "friended" them by revealing their names; i.e., long vowels. For example, in the word *each*, the *e* says its name and so is friended; the *u* in *cute* is friended. The words that contain friended vowels are circled, highlighted, or boxed. This reinforces awareness of vowels in spelling.

### GHOSTED *E*

Similar to the previous game, this one requires students to identify and highlight all the words with silent or "ghosted" examples of the letter *e*. For example, the *e* in cap*e* is ghosted. You can have students make a list of all the ghosted-*e* words they find.

### SETS AND SIMILARS

This activity is a sorting and classification exercise, as well as being a spelling reinforcer. To up the game aspect, pair students and have them race against each other. The first team that finishes wins, assuming, of course, they have all the sets correct.

1. Explain that, in pairs, students will be racing to put words in categories, or groups that fit together, based on the spelling of the words. For example, all words from the following list that have a silent *e* or that contain *sh* could form categories:

   | | |
   |---|---|
   | *make* | *short* |
   | *shall* | *care* |
   | *rake* | *she* |

   Group 1: *make, rake, care*
   Group 2: *shall, short, she*

2. Provide words in random order, being sure that specific spelling rules can be used to categorize the words; for example, silent *e*, double letters, long vowels, etc. The list can include regular spelling words, plus content-based words pulled from subject vocabulary, such as science (habitats, foods, mammals) or math (words related to addition/subtraction, geometry, fractions).
3. Start the game and play for a pre-selected amount of time or until a pair completes the task.
4. Debrief by pointing out spelling mistakes and discussing discrepancies and similarities.

### ALPHABET SOUP

In teams or pairs, students are given a list of spelling words that are scrambled. Teams race against each other to unscramble the letters and form the words.

**How-to-Wow Spelling**
- **Teach spelling in class in context.**
- **Play spelling games regularly.**
- **Draw students' attention to spelling in context all the time.**
- **Remind students of the difference between texting and in-school spelling.**

### LETTER SELECT

On index cards, write single letters, blends, and letters that represent other spelling concepts you are studying. Students in teams randomly draw a card and have three seconds to spell a word containing that letter or blend. The team scores a point for each correct word supplied within the time frame.

### DISAPPEARING FIGURE

Each team copies in pencil a stick person you have drawn with six to ten parts; e.g., head, body, neck, two arms, two legs, two feet, a hat. Teams give their figures to an opposing team. Every time a spelling word is spelled correctly, a piece of the figure's body is erased. The goal is to erase all of the competition's figures, making them disappear, before they can erase yours.

### LETTER MASH-UP

Teams or partners are given a number of random letters and race to create more words than their opponents can. Marks are awarded for correctly spelled words, and subtracted for incorrect words. You can put a time limit on the game if you wish.

### WORD SEARCH DETECTIVE

This differs slightly from the familiar word search, which is, in itself, an excellent spelling enhancement tool. Choose an answer that can be made up of the first letter of each of the words you assemble for the word search.

Answer: sun
Words in puzzle:  **s**and
          **u**nder
          **n**ose

Once all the words have been found, students take the first letters of all the found words and put them together to find the answer.

### LONELY LETTER

This game works best in teams of 4 or 5 students. Each team is given the same letter, set alone within a specific number of blanks for other letters. The goal is to make as many words as possible from the lonely letter, without moving it from its position in the sequence of blanks. For example, given __ *a* __ __, students could make *make, cake, late, tall*—any four-letter words that have an *a* in the second position. The longer the word, the more difficult; if two lonely letters are given, the game promotes higher-level thinking and spelling. For example, __*i* __ __ *t* could lead to *night, sight, limit,* etc. At the end of the set time, the team with the most correctly spelled words wins.

### TEXT VS RIGHT WRITE

This game takes a critical look at texting, the short forms it uses, and how they relate to good spelling in the classroom. As teachers, you cannot ignore the fact that your students have already developed a texting shorthand. It can, and will, interfere with good writing and spelling unless you take a stand. In Text vs Right Write, students are required to rewrite text shorthand into proper spelling.

Texting is very loose in its structure. No one thinks about spelling or grammar in texts. That's because texting is more akin to talking than writing. This important difference should be shared with students.

1. Discuss texting and the use of shorthand; e.g. "u" for "you."
2. Brainstorm the many instances of shorthand used by students. Compile them into a chart or poster.
3. In pairs, students rewrite each shorthand (or a selected number of them; there might be too many for one sitting) correctly, as they would in a literacy paper.
4. The team that finishes first wins.
5. It is important to debrief by stressing how important it is to use Right Write at school. Discuss the convenience of shorthand, and compare it to the properness of Right Write.

## Grammar

Like spelling, grammar feels like a thing of the past, a dinosaur that should be laid to rest. But should it really? Consider the following true scenario:

> A relatively new teacher was applying at a school for a position for the upcoming year. She was well-educated, clear-spoken, and properly dressed to make a good impression. She was pleasant and polite but, when asked a question by the principal, she responded, "I seen that strategy being used when I was at university."

William Somerset Maugham postulated that it is "well to remember that grammar is common speech formulated." We want our students to go forth with more than just common speech. We need to address grammar.

That single grammar slip cost her the position. Grammar, in the professional world, remains very important. It is the set of rules that governs word usage and meaning. This is a concept worth sharing with students. You can pose a situation, such as the one here, and ask them if the person should be hired; why or why not. Students need to be aware of the importance of not only what they say, but how they say it. Good grammar both in speaking and in writing is a sign of being educated.

If you have decided to include specific grammar instruction in your classroom, there are a few basics to remember. Teaching grammar, like teaching spelling, is best done in context. It may seem difficult to capture the wow factor when teaching grammar, but your personal enthusiasm and positive approach to the subject can go a long way. In addition, the use of grammar games can serve as a big wow for students.

- Have students read and write in class all the time, and encourage them do the same at home.
- Do sentence combining activities together. For example, put *the boy*, *with his dog*, and *went to the store* together in different ways:

  With his dog, the boy went to the store.
  The boy went to the store with his dog.
  To the store the boy went with his dog.

- Encourage self-editing of work. Have students read their work out loud to themselves. It's easier to find errors if you can hear what you've written.
- Draw attention to punctuation, capitals, and examples of good grammar every day in reading of texts, stories, posters, announcements, etc. Tell students to have "wise eyes" and "smart ears" when it comes to grammar.
- Use minilessons often for teachable moments when you see/hear a grammar error. Instead of thinking, "I'll come back to that later," deal with it immediately; the learning in context will be effective.

- When teaching younger students, remind yourself that teaching grammar in isolation—diagramming sentences, identifying parts of speech—is teaching grammar as it doesn't work in practice, and is a waste of your valuable time.
- Where the "No grammar as grammar" rule doesn't apply is at high school. Here grammar does need to be addressed specifically with more concrete lessons that diagram sentences, insert punctuation, identify parts of speech, etc. But even at this level, keeping it fun, lighthearted, and in context helps. A good idea is to have races in which teams compete to correctly punctuate difficult sentences.

## Grammar Games

See page 82 for more grammar games.

By now you understand how much value I put on games in a learning environment. These games help promote or reinforce basic grammar rules without actually calling them rules. In all cases, difficulty can be increased by increasing the complexity of the grammar convention you wish to address.

### GRAMMAR TIC TAC TOE

This variation on the original game can be played in pairs or teams. The object of the game is, of course, to draw a straight line between three *X*s or *O*s. The hard part is that you have to prepare the game pages ahead of time, by writing an example of the grammar rule you are studying in each of the nine squares. For example, if you are working on verb tense, squares might include *past tense of* run, *future tense of* eat, *present tense of* is. The student selects a square in which to place their X or O, but must correctly supply the word to win that square. As a team game, team members take turns choosing squares for their teams. If played as a team game, team members are allowed to coach each other (peer tutoring) and more difficult concepts can be used and reinforced.

### SAY IT RIGHT

Points are earned by students correcting aloud a grammar pattern you have presented incorrectly in a sentence. For example,

*I go see that movie tonight.*
*I go to that school during five years.*
*Thirsty need water.*
*We make car ride now.*

**This game format can be used with any grammar rules or concepts you want to reinforce.**

Teams work against each other to earn points. Two points are awarded for a correct sentence. If the team member whose turn it is requires help from the rest of the team to correct the sentence, only one point is scored. If the answer is incorrect, no points are scored.

### GRAMMAR DETECTIVES

Younger students love this game, and it involves them at home and at school. It is an individual activity, but I have seen students with partners eagerly seeking and recording examples of bad grammar. This game takes a bit of preparation so that students really know what to look for, and consequently is often used after grammar has been dealt with in class.

1. Discuss "talking right" and share examples of both good and not-so-good talk. Try to use examples that students themselves might use, such as "I done…" or "I don't got no…"

2. Point out that everywhere around us there are examples of poor grammar. Sharing images is helpful. Here are a few actually found in advertising:

   *You're ad here.* (sign)
   *Lets go blue.* (Old Navy T-shirt)
   *So much fun they won't know there learning.* (ad for educational software)
   *Perfection has it's price.* (beer ad)
   *Sport's bar* (sign)
   *Express line starts their.* (grocery store)

**How-to-Wow Grammar**
- **Teach grammar in context, all the time for younger students.**
- **Make use of teachable moments every time a grammar crisis occurs.**
- **Point out good grammar in text and oral communication.**
- **Teach awareness of poor grammar.**
- **Talk, talk, and talk about the importance of good grammar.**
- **Use grammar games to reinforce concepts.**

3. Give students the directive to find the mistakes in a given detecting period. These can be errors in punctuation, spelling, word usage, etc. Depending on the age of students, have them keep a record of the errors they find to share in class. Some students may want to take photos as well.

4. Remind students that the errors can be in overheard spoken language too. (One brave young student recorded her father saying "ain't" a total of 34 times in one detecting period.) If you want, you can limit the detecting to spoken language.

5. After about a week of detecting, debrief as a class, looking together at the errors and correcting them.

ONLINE GAMES/ACTIVITIES

There are many sites with excellent activities that reinforce grammar as you deal with it in class. Use these games not as rewards, but as tools to validate in-class learning. Many sites offer downloadable sheets or boards. One good example is Grammar Land Game Board, which reinforces grammar terms and concepts.

AGREEABLE VERBS

This game for pairs reinforces subject/verb agreement, a basic grammar rule taught from an early level. Use index cards, writing subjects on half and verbs on the other half. One student holds the subjects; the other holds the verbs. They take turns blindly drawing cards from each other. If they get an appropriate match, they lay down that pair. If they can't make a match, the picked card goes in to a pile in the middle. Once all cards in the hands are used, players draw from the middle until no more matches can be made. For example, subject *Men* verb *Plays*. Obviously "men plays" doesn't work, so this is not a matching pair. The player with the most matches wins.

PIN THE PART

Once students have a basic understanding of the four main parts of speech (noun, verb, adjective, adverb), this simple game reinforces the concept. Make a large box shape on a chart or the board. Divide it into quadrants labeled *Noun*, *Verb*, *Adjective*, and *Adverb*. In teams, students take turns lifting a card from a face-down pile of index cards on which are written examples of the four parts of speech. The student has three seconds to pin the word in the correct box. If they are right, the team gets a mark. If wrong, the other team gets a chance at the same word. The team with the most points wins.

JOB INTERVIEW

This activity involves role play as well as grammar awareness. Plus, one student gets to be the "bad guy," always a popular role. Directions are a little complicated, but the final role plays do an excellent job or reinforcing good speaking grammar.

1. Break students into groups of three or four.
2. Present the scene. Two students in each team are being interviewed for a job at a fast-food restaurant. Student A has experience but speaks with bad grammar and slang. Student B has no experience but speaks well.
3. The interviewer (and helper) ask questions of both candidates.
4. Following the interview, the employers discuss the two candidates. They must decide who they choose to hire and support their choice to the rest of the class.
5. If students choose the person using poor grammar, point out how this would probably work in real life; i.e., The better-spoken person would get hired.
6. Debrief by discussing the impact our spoken language has on others.

"Grammar is a piano, and I play by ear." — Joan Didion

The quote in the margin sums up what we already know about grammar. It becomes second nature. We don't think about it. It just exists as a part of our communication system. But what happens when it doesn't work right, when poor grammar interferes with communication and with how others see us? When adults use incorrect grammar it is much more difficult to fix than when children do the same, so let's encourage good grammar now. I share a final true story:

> When I was supervising student teachers, one young lady was filled with enthusiasm, excited about the students, obviously intelligent, and ready to teach. However, she used terrible grammar, saying things like "I don't got no…," "I seen," "I done," etc. After my first time observing her, we talked at length about this problem. She seemed genuinely surprised. Why had no one ever pointed this out to her before? I wondered the same thing. I would like to report that she mastered her problem; I know she tried. But after her student teaching placement I never heard from her again. All I can say is that, if she continued to speak so poorly, I wouldn't have wanted her teaching my child.

## The Wow of Teaching Themes

Using a thematic approach in the classroom is not a novel idea, but today, more than ever, it is perhaps the best way to prepare students to be successful in a highly technological society. What is taught by the curriculum is not arbitrary. Nor can it be watered down or overlooked. But the way in which it is presented and delivered to students is entirely up to you. If we want to develop students' ability to behave proactively in an ever-changing world, we need to offer more than bare bones curriculum. And we need to offer it with the wow factor included if we want to compete with the immediate gratification offered by technology. One good way to do that is to use a thematic approach, connecting together many areas of the mandated curriculum with a theme, and thus providing a more elemental and less fragmented approach that is generally more motivating and interesting for students.

Teaching themes is an example of the interdisciplinary strategy mentioned in Chapter 3, but thematic involvement can be either minor or major, depending on the needs/interests of your class.

The use of a thematic approach has inherent wow. Students will be studying a common area of interest and every detail, regardless of the subject area being examined, will be more powerful. Think of the theme as being a warm blanket that is holding all the content together. That's wow! You will see the wow in the eyes of your students daily. Why use themes?

- Students follow a thread of learning that flows from one subject to another. This teaches them about relationships and is a lifelong learning skill.
- It is fun and motivating for students to do their own seek-and-search for theme-related topics and issues, which they then share with the class. It encourages confidence and feelings of self-worth.
- Students make connections, transfer knowledge, and use strategies, such as comparison and categorization, automatically.
- When students with different abilities all share the same theme, a sense of community develops.

Most frequently, themes are limited to literacy studies, perhaps with a sprinkling of health matters thrown in. In primary grades especially, themes are often short-lived focuses on specific days and/or holidays. Although this is still a thematic approach, I suggest a bit broader use of the theme idea. The best themes help create lifelong learners who are able to critically think about and discuss big ideas and concepts. Remember, the more you expect of your students, the more you will receive. So let's think big when it comes to choosing study themes.

## Theme Identification

The theme is very important and should reflect both student interest and a significant social problem or issue.

1. Begin by sharing that together you will choose a theme. Explain what this means to students.
2. Open a class discussion about topics of interest. At first, allow random sharing (hands raised) of anything and everything that interests students.
3. You (or a student assigned the task) jot down single words as students share. These words will be reviewed when it comes to narrowing the field.
4. Review the many ideas together and ask if students can see a way to clump similar ideas together.
5. Try to organize little ideas into bigger, more social ideas, such as bullying, friendship, saving the environment, good health, sharing, confidence, etc. If you already have a theme in mind, you can use your teacher smarts to mold students' ideas toward your theme. For instance, a Grade 2 class listed as their interests *friends, family, superheroes, sports, games, pets, dancing, winning at games, camping, hiking, outdoor activities*. Their teacher had been hoping to get to a theme that somehow showed individual strengths in the face of difficulties. After careful study of the varied list, the teacher suggested the word *power*, and showed the students how it worked with many of their suggestions.

## Theme Development

1. Have students all create something that will show off their new theme. This could be a piece of writing, a poster, a drawing, a cartoon strip, a song—whatever they want to create. Display their creations.
2. Invest some time in skimming curriculum objectives in core subjects and identifying those you wish to cover. Make a chart or list of these and fit them into your theme. This sounds harder than it is, and not all curriculum objectives need to fit the theme.

"Pick a theme and work it to exhaustion...the subject must be something you truly love or truly hate." — Dorothea Lang

Using a thematic approach is not for everyone. For some of you, and for some students, a partial theme may be enough. In this case you still identify a theme, but don't necessarily tie all content learning to it.

"Today you are you. That is truer than true. There is no one alive who is youer than you!" — Dr. Seuss

Brad Henry says, "A good teacher can inspire hope, ignite the imagination, and instill a love of learning." A good theme, under the guidance of a good teacher, can do the same.

3. Create a large presentation area where the theme name is proudly displayed, together with student offerings. This should be a constantly changing display, showing different subject/theme-related tasks done by students.
4. Continually draw work back to the theme. Depending on your theme, this might be done in just a few well-chosen words. For example, using the Power theme, during a math lesson about fractions the teacher commented, "Learning how to manipulate fractions is a super power."

## Sample Themes

You will develop the theme on its own by having separate minilessons directly related to the theme content while, as the curriculum readily adapts, tying other subjects to the theme. Whatever approach you use, it's useful to have a list of possible themes that have proven effective for other teachers.

- All About Me: At first glance this seems like a Grade 1 or Kindergarten theme, but students of all ages love talking about themselves. Older students will take an approach that differs from that taken by younger children, but the theme is just as important and productive.
- Animal Theme (animals in general or a specific animal): I saw this theme used at high-school level: students themselves were expected to tie all their core courses to the theme by journaling, writing, or creating projects or posters. Because they had different teachers for every subject, their skills for comparison, categorization, and compilation were tested. They loved it!
- Country/Continent: This is another common theme, with a single country being selected in most cases. And that country is very student-specific. For example, a Grade 3 class had a new student from England, so decided to use England as a theme so that they could learn more about her home land. Another class, after several students had watched a distressing news piece about Mexican refugees, chose Mexico as a theme.
- Movement: This is a beautiful, broad theme that allows expansion in many directions. It was suggested by a boy who broke his leg and was complaining about his lack of movement. Another student wisely said, "I guess we don't appreciate movement until we can't move." Another child added, "But there are other ways to move besides walking." And the theme Movement was born.
- Vacations: This is an easy theme right after a holiday such as spring break, especially if some lucky children have actually traveled to somewhere special. It can be general or specific to a type of location (e.g., beach, mountains, camping). A Grade 6 class used Camping as a theme and finished the theme with a real camping trip to a nearby lake.
- Pop Culture: Adolescents love this one. They are creative at fitting a wide variety of learning experiences into the arms of this theme, so in fact, a lot of your work is done for you. One class actually sent online letters to a pop star and received a note back. They earned enough money, through bake sales, yard sales, and community work, to go as a class to a pop concert in a neighboring city. They created a School Pop Culture Handbook that contained school-related information about music, sports, leisure activities, fads, etc.

The list of themes is endless: health, community, construction, fantasy, emotions, science fiction, friendship, growing things, mindfulness, monsters, weather, transportation, space, Middle Earth. You and you students will come up with themes that are special and important to you. Use a theme and experience some of the wow of teaching.

# Chapter 3 Teaching Strategies

**How-to-Wow Teaching Strategies**
- Familiarize yourself with a variety of strategies.
- Connect a chosen strategy to your lesson objective.
- Prepare all that is required for that strategy.
- Introduce the strategy and the objective to the class.
- Remain open-minded. Other strategies may slip into play. Go with it.
- Close by summarizing and pointing out how the strategy used facilitated learning.

Are you are a lecturer? Or perhaps a discussion leader or a ready questioner? Do you prefer students to work individually or in groups? These are indications of your teaching style. Your style will depend on what is natural and easy for you; it is a reflection of your personality. On the other hand, strategies are learned and developed over time. For strategies to be effective, a variety of ideas, methods, tips, and suggestions must be integrated. This chapter will suggest an assortment of strategies and supply cues and clues to implement them. Keep in mind that teacher-led strategies will become independent-learning strategies and life strategies for your students, and that the more and varied your strategies are, the more you are training independent learners.

Literally dozens of teaching strategies have developed over the years, been popular, then slipped into obscurity. Recall the 1980s excitement about "open classrooms in circular schools"? How well did that strategy work? What strategies you use today will depend on your personal style, your familiarity with a variety of different strategies, and your skill in using them effectively. By choosing the right strategy for specific learning, you are paying attention to detail to create something meaningful and memorable for your students. The strategy should have distinctive appeal. The right strategy will capture students' attention and incite their interest and curiosity, creating that important wow factor for both you and your class.

A strategy is a way to teach, and you will develop ones that work for you if you haven't already. As a rule, they are blueprints configured by you in advance, with the hope of reaching specific objectives. A good teaching strategy is as much choosing what not to do as it is choosing what you will do. As a framework of what to do, it is comforting reassurance that what you are doing as a teacher is wise, premeditated, and proven to be effective. Thus, using a strategy takes away some of the gray area of how-to in teaching. There is no way to teach without using strategies (even lecturing is using a strategy, albeit a rather boring one), so having an awareness of some of the most popular ones, as well as suggestions for their use, can be helpful.

There are what I refer to as grand strategies, those that incorporate the entire class for a considerable amount of time—more than one lesson, perhaps even an entire unit. Then there are the everyday strategies, the smaller, daily activities that slip under the umbrellas of the grand strategies and work within them. You can use several of these lesser strategies in a single lesson. Each strategy in this chapter is described in practical terms, and a simple step-by-step version of how to use it is included.

# Grand Strategies

## Cooperative Learning

This is essentially the formation of groups in which members work together for a shared result. Group work is so familiar to teachers that it has been listed first. Many other strategies can be incorporated into the realm of cooperative learning or group work. Within this framework, students learn from each other.

Why group work?

- Students gain cooperation and sharing skills.
- Students learn from each other.
- Students are engaged in face-to-face activities, which promotes healthy interaction.
- Students are held accountable for each other, as the group is given a single evaluation.
- Students get practice in both good listening skills and good questioning techniques.
- Students experience delegation of responsibility.
- Students gain experience in interpersonal and social interaction.

"It is literally true that you can succeed best and quickest by helping others to succeed." — Napoleon Hill

### Forming Groups

It is important to be able to establish groups quickly. If you are grouping for specific skill instruction, assign students to groups and quickly tell students what part of the room to move to. In many cases it is good to group students randomly, maintaining a variety of personalities and abilities in each group to ensure maximum learning from peers. Tell students that groupings are going to be random. Any of the following work quickly and efficiently:

- counting off: the tried and true method of quick group formulation. If you constantly change your starting point, groups will not always be the same. Rather than numbers you can group from a list pertinent to recent learning, such as *Canada, Russia, China, India, Mexico* and have students repeat in order; all the *Canada*s form one group, and so on.
- using first letters of names
- name length: e.g., names with 4 or fewer letters, with 5 to 7 letters, etc.
- drawing items; e.g., sticks, colored toothpicks, colored or numbered pieces of paper, etc.
- word cards: random draw of words where groups of words mean the same thing (e.g., *cold, chilly, frozen, icy, frigid*); students group with their synonyms
- playing cards: group by color, suit, or number/face of cards
- word puzzles: words pertinent to classroom activities or studies on index cards are cut into as many parts as you want groups. For example you could cut *ecosystem* into *eco, sy, st, em*; students group according to the complete words.

### Working in Groups Using GAIN

It's true that not all students work as well in groups as others. But when you look at the big picture, unless one is planning to live as a hermit, the ability to work within the confines of a group is a mandatory human skill. Providing students

Share this acronym with students and make it visible throughout group time. Use the word *GAIN* to indicate that they gain a great deal from helping and working with peers.

with in-class group work is a teaching strategy that works on many levels. To make group work succeed, you need to begin by getting attention, then establishing a few rules. You can follow the steps of GAIN: **G**et ready; **A**ll must contribute; **I**ndividuals do what they are best at; **N**otes kept at every stage.

1. **G**et ready: form your group and bring necessary materials for the project.
2. **A**ll group members must contribute. Share the work. Be cooperative.
3. **I**ndividuals do what they are best at doing.
4. **N**otes must be kept at every stage of your work so that you can quickly return to it another day.

A little pre-teaching of how to work in groups goes a long way. Before you get students into groups, discuss as a class what makes for a good group experience and what doesn't, then summarize these points quickly for them as soon as the groups are together. A visual of group-work *do*s and *don't*s can be a helpful reminder too.

Effective group work must be guided and shaped. It isn't a time for the teacher to sit aside and mark papers or plan lessons. You need to be visible and in control at all times, even with older, more self-sufficient students. Follow these steps for perfect group management.

1. Determine exactly where each group will get together.
2. Clearly communicate each group goal or objective. Make these visible as well as auditory.
3. Have decided which method you will use to group (see page 51).
4. Have all necessary materials on hand at each group station.
5. Tell students when to start. Remind them when it is close to stop time. Provide a ten-minute warning.
6. Monitor by circulating constantly. Be visible.
7. Provide a rubric for evaluation of the group's work. This will reflect the goal of the group. Give this to students as a guide for work.
8. Provide a group checklist for students to use to keep a running record of who did what. Students quickly learn to divide up the work and can initial beside the roles they choose. Keep these checklists as a teaching tool to track which students continually choose the same role so you can encourage variation in what students do.

## Inquiry-Based Instruction

How-to-Wow Inquiry-Based Instruction
• Present the problem or situation.
• Discuss possible ways to proceed.
• During individual work time, check for appropriateness of pursuits.
• Review, share, debrief.

In this teaching strategy, students are encouraged to learn by doing. This paradigm has teachers as facilitators; students are explorers and seekers. It is an excellent strategy when incorporated with other learning strategies, but on its own it has presented some difficulties. There are different types of inquiry but, for the purposes of this book, I have simplified them by considering inquiry as a single strategy. The pros and cons of isolated (i.e., not mixed with other strategies) inquiry instruction are laid out here:

PROS

- Students are engaged in the learning process.
- Students explore topics of interest deeply and learn from experiences.
- Students take ownership of their own learning.

CONS

- Testing and evaluation for progress is difficult.
- It is almost impossible to measure the creativity and critical thinking required of the strategy.
- Teamwork is important to this strategy, and not all students like to work, or work well, in groups.
- The lack of structure can be disruptive, especially for some students; this creates a difficult teaching/learning situation.

"Doubt comes in at the window when inquiry is denied at the door." — Benjamin Jowett

Although at first glance there seem to be more cons than pros, many teachers make inquiry work well. However, since it has been shown that inquiry-based instruction is best integrated with many other strategies, that is the focus assumed here. In this way you can better reach all students and offer many game plans for life in the process. To be effective, inquiry-based instruction must take into consideration students' needs and curiosities, at the same time as sticking to the mandated curriculum. This can be a tough road to follow, and may be feasible for only specific subject areas. However, as a teacher, you know that progress is born from doubt and inquiry, so encouraging inquiry is a part of your professional obligation. So, let's use the inquiry method in the best way(s) possible.

1. Explain the problem to students, making sure they all understand it. Clearly speak it, write it, review it, and ask them for clarification. (Use the tips for clear directions on page 32.)
2. Have each student make their own plan. Tell them the plan can be written, illustrated, jotted in point form, graphed—as long as it is understandable to them and can be followed and reviewed. For many students, creating a list of steps is the easiest plan.
3. Have students list their resources: where/whom/how they will pursue and research their topics.
4. Find a way to review each student's plan of attack before they go any further. You might choose to have a five-minute interview with each student, on a rotating basis, carried out while the class is otherwise involved. Keep it short. All you are doing is determining if the student is on the right track and has a good idea regarding resources.
5. Tell students to proceed with the first part of their plans and move as quickly or slowly as they need through the steps as they carry out their individual plans.
6. Encourage students to continually look back and evaluate as they move forward with their plans.
7. Share finished projects with you or peers.

Use the inquiry strategy together with other teaching strategies, such as whole-class discussion or group work, for best results.

## Portfolio Development

Portfolios are usually a collection of materials gathered for proof of accomplishment, and sometimes can be presented online as digital or e-portfolios. But as a classroom strategy, a portfolio is a hard-copy collection of student tasks and gatherings related to a specific topic. The final product is generally a source of student pride and, consequently, filled with the wow factor. Gathering the elements for this type of portfolio is both engaging and motivating for students once they clearly understand what is expected. Using the portfolio strategy can help students develop an understanding of what portfolios are and how they can be

How-to-Wow Portfolio Strategy
- **Choose and discuss a topic or theme.**
- **Choose a receptacle.**
- **Share a model portfolio.**
- **Hand out student checklists.**
- **Review resources.**
- **Allow class time; do periodic checks.**
- **Share.**

helpful in the future. For this kind of portfolio, students will gather items and/or pieces of work related to a topic of study, a random selection of student-chosen best pieces of work in any subject, or a selection of literacy-based work—whatever you want it to be.

With this strategy, you need to have a goal in mind; e.g., everything related to our animal study in science, all the writing you do from now until the end of the year, etc. Discuss with students what kinds of things can go in the portfolio, as well as what sort of container they might want to use—binders, scrapbooks, photo albums, art books—and any number of odds and ends, such as stickers and ribbons. Of course, if a flat folder container is used, the student will be limited to two-dimensional (flat) objects. With younger students, shoe boxes are preferable, as much of what students want to include will be three-dimensional.

What sorts of things can go into a student portfolio? If the portfolio has no theme and is a collection of students' work, any and all of the following can be included. If there is a theme, the following can still be used as long as they can be fitted to the theme in some way:

- journal entries: very important—student's daily log regarding the portfolio
- artwork
- awards or certificates
- clippings from magazines or newspapers
- photos
- tests, quizzes
- writing examples
- questions with answers
- interviews
- charts and illustrations

Why use the portfolio strategy?

- Students take ownership over their own learning.
- Students are motivated: they collect and reflect within their own interest frames.
- The end products are useful for evaluation purposes.
- The portfolios can be ongoing, and be developed at the same time as other strategies are being used.
- Portfolios are great communication devices for parents and teachers.
- Portfolios are fun!

If you use the portfolio strategy, setting it up carefully will enable students to move ahead on their own with relative ease. It's true the creation of portfolios can be daunting and can take a lot of teacher time and effort, but this doesn't have to be the case. If you keep it simple and use the following steps, you can make the portfolio strategy work for you.

1. Introduce the idea by sharing a finished or partly finished portfolio. The use of a model is very important.
2. Provide an outline of steps for students to follow. It might look like this:

   a. Find a shoe box or other similar box (or a folder, binder, etc.). Label it with the defining topic.
   b. Write your name on the portfolio.

A shoebox portfolio created by younger children is an excellent display for parent viewing or even full-school viewing. The boxes can be presented on tables in the hall or in the classroom, where other classes can be invited to see the amazing collections.

c. Start by putting little things that relate to the defining topic in your box/folder.

d. Write a short story/sentence/paragraph about each item, explaining why you chose it.

e. Keep your portfolio at home/at your desk/on the shelf/etc.

3. Have a class discussion about what sorts of items might go into the portfolio.

4. Begin immediately: the first step before collection begins is a written description or illustration (for younger children) of what the portfolio is all about. This will be the first thing to go into the portfolio; this constitutes the portfolio theme.

5. Proceed with a lesson specifically related to the portfolios. For example, if your portfolios are science-based, dealing with ecosystems of the Alberta natural foothills region, teach a lesson based on the core element of topic.

## Learning Logs for Reflection

A learning log, like a diary or journal, is personal writing done by the student in response to everyday school experiences. The difference from the point of view of the teacher is, however, that while a journal or diary is private and the child can rightfully decide not to share, a learning log is designed to be shared with the teacher and used for support and learning. They are collections of personal responses, brief summaries of what has been learned, difficulties, achievements, and evidence to support claims. They show evolution of knowledge and confidence over time.

As a strategy, learning logs can be used as reflective tools for both student and teacher. This strategy can work with all ages; however, it becomes more efficient once students can write well. Younger pre-readers can still create learning logs using diagrams and drawings in response to teacher-orated questions. Students use learning logs to record notes following specific lessons throughout the day. Learning logs should be factual, largely objective (i.e., less emotional content), and concise. They can be strictly related to a particular course or to learning in general. It has been found that the best results from learning logs come when there is some structure provided, when there are questions that students can choose to answer, for example:

- What did I learn in _____ (subject)?
- Why was it interesting or not interesting?
- What did I have trouble with?
- What do I need help with?
- What am I looking forward to in _____ (subject) in the future?
- Do I like/dislike this class? Why?

If you have decided to use learning logs in your classroom, there are a few thoughts to keep in mind.

Sharing a learning log you made yourself (create one for anything new you have learned; make it humorous as well as serious) is an excellent motivational tool. Students love to see what their teacher has done.

1. Decide whether the log is to be subject-related or general.
2. Create a few sample entries as a model. Share them with the class.
3. Provide the journals.
4. Discuss together the list of possible guide questions. Chart them or have them easily available.

5. Allow students time immediately for personal reflections on how the logs might proceed.
6. Remember to regularly allow time for entries.
7. Since these are learning logs, set up times for individuals to share with you so that together you can follow up where necessary.

## Whole-Class Discussion

Group discussions are an integral part of life. In the classroom, they are a strategy that provides students with an audience for ideas and allows them to hear and reflect on the ideas of others. Unfortunately, in most group discussions, there are a few students who like to take over and a few who remain silent. As an open-minded teacher you need to accept this situation, but at the same time try to steer the discussion to include everyone—not an easy task. It might be helpful to share the following quote and discuss its meaning.

"Discussion is an exchange of knowledge. Argument an exchange of ignorance."
— Robert Quillan

All teachers know the importance of whole-class discussion, but sometimes getting it to play out smoothly is easier said than done.

1. Start by creating a classroom of fairness and respect. If you talk with your class about this and model it, students will follow.
2. Establish a few discussion rules. They might look like this:

  - No put downs.
  - Let others talk too.
  - Ask questions of each other.
  - Listen carefully.
  - No interrupting.
  - Anyone can choose to pass; i.e., not answer or speak when asked.

3. Conduct a trial discussion about a topic of common interest.
4. Always have in mind a few productive questions that will get students thinking if/when conversation stops. Your job as mediator is to keep things going.
5. Stop after a few minutes and evaluate. Ask students how they felt it went. Express your own feelings about it.
6. Model summarizing concisely what was discussed. Tell students that in the future you will expect them to summarize themselves.
7. The next time you want to have a class discussion, remind students of the rules and the trial discussion. Tell them, "This is a real discussion. Play your part well." Often, if students are reminded you are having a discussion, as opposed to merely chatting, they will become more aware and serious.

## Interdisciplinary Instruction

For this strategy, the teacher creates lessons and involves students in such a way that products and activities are related to more than one subject. In other words, science concepts can be included in the reading skills discussion, or a counting game can be used in physical education. You are asking yourself, "Don't all teachers do that all the time?" Most certainly many teachers do, but the true art of interdisciplinary teaching goes a bit further. Under the umbrella of this grand strategy, no subject is taught in isolation. That's a tough act but, when it is successful, it is filled with wow.

Chances are you won't be involved in a total interdisciplinary approach, but I include it as a suggestion for some of your teaching. An example for young children would be to read (literacy) about a science concept, listen (literacy) to the teacher read about it, illustrate (art) some part of the concept, write (literacy) a short paragraph about the concept, measure or count (math) the components of the concept, and discuss the understanding of the concept at different times (social studies). In this way, more than one discipline is being taught.

1. Think about an area of study you will be covering, based on curriculum.
2. Brainstorm ideas for pursuing it using different tactics and disciplines.
3. Use graphic organizers to plot connections between the specific area of study and other core areas. Keep referring to curriculum objectives.
4. List several objectives that incorporate all the disciplines you plan to use.
5. Create your lesson with the multidisciplinary approach in mind. The first time you do this, it will be cumbersome, but it does get easier with practice.
6. Present the overall project to students, who will likely be excited by the novelty of the project.
7. Create a linear approach for yourself, but be open-minded. Students may take off in many directions once motivated.
8. Keep referring back to your curriculum-based objectives. Are they being met? If not, how can you change the approach to meet them? It might take no more than a few minilessons. Don't let overzealousness about the strategy take you too far from your original goal(s).

**Invite students to determine how a particular theme, topic, or unit of study could be spread over various disciplines. For example, if you are studying global warming, ask how it could be related to literacy, math, health, even physical education. Then use their ideas.**

## Everyday Strategies

These are the schemes, systems, and tactics that teachers use every day, often with little or no pre-thought. Some might be unfamiliar. The way some strategies can be used might be novel. Your own skills and intuition will tell you how each everyday strategy helps students learn and grow. It's important to debrief following every strategy used; debriefing can vary from a simple question "What did you learn/experience/remember/feel/etc.?" to a written essay or report.

### Role-Play Strategies

**"Every one of us has been called to be an actor in the drama of life, and everyone has a role to play as well."**
**— Myra Yadav**
**Play your role(s) well.**

Role play is an authentic learning activity in which students are actively involved. It builds confidence and enhances communication development. Depending on exactly what students are playing, it can involve problem-solving (e.g., acting out a bullying situation), facts review (e.g., acting out a history lesson), etc. We are all actors, teachers and students alike, and, as the quote in the margin suggests, playing our roles well is what will lead to ultimate success. By giving students chances to try different hats and play different roles, we are giving them life experiences.

For this strategy, the roles the teacher must play include narrator, producer, director, and prompter. If you play your roles well, the students will play theirs well too.

1. Choose an objective for the role play. It can be based on a recent happening, a story read together, a specific situation witnessed or shared, etc.
2. Explain the problem, setting, and characters to the students. Keep it open-ended; don't provide a solution. Students will come up with their own.
3. Share your expectations just as you would for any lesson.
4. Allow practice time. This can vary depending on the age of the students, the degree of involvement, and the nature of the role play. You need to provide a time line for them, so use your best guess. The practice is merely to help students feel comfortable with their roles. Remember that the best role plays are spontaneous.
5. If students get stuck and don't know what to say/do, side coach. Be ready with general prompting questions, such as

> How is your character feeling? How can you show that?
> What might your character want to do about...?
> Can you show what your character is thinking by your actions and words?
> Let us know what your character wants/likes/hates/is annoyed about/is frustrated by.

6. Let students who do not want to act work on an alternative task at the same time. Depending on age, this could be a written or drawing assignment.
7. Share all the role plays. Remind students of how to be polite observers.
8. Debrief. Students need time to define what they have done/learned/concluded. Again, according to age and development levels, this might be an essay, a report, a story, a picture, etc.
9. Assessment is usually subjective and consists of ongoing reflective comments, such as "You are doing a good job of showing us how the characters felt/dealt with/reacted to." More formative assessment can be done at the debriefing stage if you wish.

## Games Strategies

All students love games. In fact, simply using the word "game" can be highly motivating. Here are classroom games that can be used as minor strategies to enforce or develop a concept or objective. Not all are true games, in that there are no winners or losers, but all are fun and student-centred. Of course, any student who doesn't want to be involved can pass and take an alternative assignment instead. You'll probably find that passing won't happen often when students realize the alternative activity is much less fun.

One thing to keep in mind when you announce a game is the idea that to children, games mean winners and losers. This is a good time to remind them that, particularly in these classroom games, it's not just about winning, but about being involved and having fun. Play these games with confidence that students are learning and having fun at the same time.

### Pro/Con Game

A partners game in which two sides of a situation are debated.

1. Students play in pairs. Each partner chooses a pro or con role. (Roles will switch halfway through.)

**Invite students to take a few minutes to figure out how many roles they play in life, and to illustrate or write about them.**

**You can get a lot of mileage out of referring to any classroom activity as a game. Students may realize the lunacy of this, but even then be amused (and motivated) by it. It's all about your presentation of the idea.**

**"Never let the fear of striking out keep you from playing the game."**
**— Babe Ruth**

2. Provide students a topic worth debating. This can be based on current learning in any subject. For example, the value of learning multiplication tables when we have easy access to calculators; why we should be serious about global warming.
3. Set a timer for about 5 minutes. Tell students to begin presenting their cases.
4. At the end of the set time, students change roles and repeat.
5. Debrief

## Real Game Show

An amusing take on TV game shows that allows students to overact and laugh at each other while learning.

1. Quickly discuss TV game shows.
2. Introduce your Real Game Show by choosing an MC (volunteer), team players (4–6), and an audience. (Roles can switch after a set time)
3. Provide the MC with a set of flashcards of questions related to a specific learning the class has had. For example, math cards, spelling cards, fact cards, etc.
4. Tell the players that the first person to click their fingers/smack the desk/raise a hand/etc. (you can be creative and supply clickers or small whistles) will be the first to answer. If they get the answer right, a point is awarded; if the answer is wrong, a point is subtracted.
5. Tally points and declare a winner, but be sure to remind students the game is primarily about reviewing in a fun manner.
6. Debrief.

## Erroneous Interview

This is a simple game in which a student interviewer asks questions and, in groups, students give both ridiculous answers and the real answers. Both the real answer and imaginary answer should be shared with equal passion. Remind students of game-show catch phrases, such as "And the survey says…" and "Come on down!" Tell them you are going to make your game show as ridiculous as possible. The goal of the game is to convince the show producer (the teacher) that your stance is the best one. Obviously this is a subjective decision, but the fun is in the game and the persuasive measures, not in the winning.

1. Discuss game shows in general—very quickly.
2. Explain that in this game show, you are the producer who has a lump sum of money to spend in the area that is best supported by a group. The group doesn't have to have a proper stance; it can be a ridiculous stance (e.g., for a discussion of homelessness: every household should take home a homeless person to live with them; the city zoo should be revamped to create a shelter for the homeless.) Whether the stance is real or ridiculous, students still get experience debating and supporting an issue, as well as seeing several sides to an existing problem.
3. Break the class into groups of 4 or 5 and share the theme of the topic to be discussed in the interview.
4. Allow 5 minutes for each group to brainstorm ideas together and decide on their stance. They need to come up with a strong defense to opposing ideas.

5. Discuss good interviewing techniques; e.g., avoid questions with yes/no responses. Maybe brainstorm a few good question prompts:

How do you feel about…?
What makes you think that…?
What steps do you think you will take to…?
Please explain your position on…
If you could make any changes, what would they be?

6. Choose an interviewer, either volunteer or teacher-chosen. If the latter, choose a student who is confident and has good verbal skills. You can change interviewers several times if necessary. Some students are experts at interviewing; others are more comfortable being the interviewees. Both parties learn equally well.

7. Provide a list of questions you want the interviewer to ask, or leave the questions entirely up to the interviewer. If you want to focus your interview activity on recently studied material, it's better if you have at least some of the questions ready; for example, "What would you do if you came upon a homeless person near your home?" could be a lead question following a social studies unit on community. Whichever direction you choose, be sure your interviewer has command over the situation. It's always a good idea to model as the first interviewer.

8. The interviewer asks the same question(s) to several groups so that the entire class can witness different responses. How the interviewer conducts this part of the activity will depend on the topic and the strength of the interviewer.

9. Stop and summarize as needed. For example, you might say, "It seems like group 3 is against the idea of free shelter for the homeless, while group 1 feels it is important. I wonder how group 1 would fund this?" By throwing in your summaries and suggestions, you can keep students on track and gently lead them in whatever direction you want.

10. Stop when you feel time is appropriate. As producer, choose a position to support. Remember it's not necessary to choose the most realistic stance. Rather, choose the group that did the best job of defending their position. Explain why you chose this group.

11. Debrief by discussing interviewing techniques and ways to defend personal positions. This is a strategy that can morph into many literacy-based follow ups.

## Team Bee Challenge

"Alone we can do so little; together we can do so much." — Helen Keller

Based on the idea of a spelling bee, this game makes use of team cooperation to learn, discover, master a skill, or remember factual materials. Teams are all given the same material to research or learn. Then teams play off against each other for points. The way in which points are earned depends on the age of the students and the specific challenge; usually giving points per correct response, as in a spelling bee, works. It is up to you to put together the questions for the challenge, allowing you the perfect way to check students' understanding of topics in a non-threatening manner. Play the game and reinforce learning—the perfect pair!

1. Break the class into as evenly matched teams as possible.
2. Have teams come up with team names to add to the game dimension.

3. Tell them the topic of query and point teams in the right directions for study/research.
4. Make game day a big thing. Be excited! Your enthusiasm will be contagious.
5. Call out a question to one team. They have 5 seconds to answer correctly. Have students answer in turn, the order determined by where they are sitting.
6. Scoring the game: Correct answer = 2 points. Partially correct answer = 1 point. Wrong answer = 0 points. If no response after 5 seconds, the question goes to the other team.
7. During the game, team members can pass to another team member; this removes anxiety for weaker players and puts more responsibility of stronger ones. The weaker will learn from the stronger.
8. At the end of a set time, tally points and announce a winning team
9. Award the winning team something special, such as 10 minutes free time. Try to arrange it so a different team wins the next time. It is advantageous to maintain the same teams for several games, as students learn to work well together.
10. Debrief after each game.

## Visual Strategies

### Using Visuals

**This could have been included as grand strategy because you can make it the entire focus of your teaching, and indeed, some teachers do.**

This strategy represents your attempt to bring everything you teach to life, to make it real for your students, by incorporating visuals, charts, items of interest, etc. The use of actual visuals, or tangibles, is a strategy often incorporated into various styles and types of lesson. Even a dull math lesson can come alive if you incorporate a few real-life objects. For example, when teaching about fractions, bring a bag of treats (M&Ms, small wrapped candies) use them to illustrate (the red ones equal half of the total amount), then hand out the "teaching tools" for consumption; when talking about historical dates, don an old-fashioned hat for the lesson. The ideas are limitless. Keep an open mind and be aware of your surroundings so that even the smallest, most mundane objects, such as the jar of pencils on your desk, become potential visuals and/or manipulatives.

EXAMPLES OF CONCRETE VISUALS
- charts: pie charts, histograms, line charts, area charts, scatter plots.
- diagrams, graphic organizers
- brought items of interest relating to lesson goals/objectives
- slides, Piktochart info-graphic representation online (https://piktochart.com/blog/new-theme-infographic-and-poster-templates-for-backtoschool/)
- templates
- pictures, posters, picture-book pages, calendar pages

**Using visuals with students actually *in* them (e.g., photographs used with permission) are the best possible graphic or pictorializations for student motivation.**

There is an endless supply of items and pictures that can be used for instant in class visuals. If you keep a supply of old calendars, figurines, trinkets, odds and ends, etc. in your room, your ingenuity will find a way to use them. Age is irrelevant when it comes to being motivated and stimulated by a tangible object. For a lecture on the importance of complete lesson plans, I pulled out my key chain on which there was an adorable little silvery teddy bear who was missing his legs (they had somehow fallen off). "He is not complete," I said with exaggerated sadness, "He needs legs to finish him off, just like your lessons need _____ to be complete." A few years later I met one of my ex-students, by then a teacher in his own right, and he confided that he never forgot that pathetic little legless teddy and consequently never forgot to close his lessons correctly. So always think, how can I *show* as well as *talk* this concept?

## Literal Visualization

For this strategy, students visualize, or see something in their minds as a means of comprehension and clarification. It can be taught to students as a powerful teaching tool and a valuable learning blueprint. Visualization can be used at every age and for every subject; its use will most certainly simplify your job as instructor.

EXAMPLES OF VISUALIZATION

1. Individual visualization: paragraph, story, science fact, historical fact, mathematics problem, etc.
2. Visualizations for specific real-life situations: e.g., when a bully is threatening you
3. Visualizations for study purposes: reviewing content by visualizing it and seeing basic concepts

Like any teaching strategy, students must be shown, or taught, how and when to use visualization effectively. Remember that when you teach students learning strategies, you are actually teaching life strategies as well.

1. Model the strategy. For example: *When I close my eyes I can picture those days long ago. There is a dusty street and...*
2. Have students do the same for another portion or selection: *Close your eyes and try to see... We will share following.* Other lead statements could be

   *Pretend you are making a movie of... What do you see/need?*
   *Think of colorful adjectives and verbs to describe what you see.*
   *Pretend you are looking through a crystal ball. What do you see happening?*
   *"In your mind, see all the main points of..."*

3. Share the visualizations.
4. If students have accurate visualizations, compliment them and indicate why they are accurate. For example, "You saw a covered wagon. That would absolutely be in that time and place."
5. If students are off-base, question further to assess accountability: "Explain why you saw that. Where in the paragraph/story/essay/lesson did you see that?" (this is a test of comprehension). Repeat a visualization of your own as a model; repeat task.
6. Follow up by discussing where/how this strategy might be used in daily life. Perhaps make a chart that could include ideas:

   - thinking in your mind where in a store you will look for something
   - planning a birthday party for outside
   - deciding which route to ride your bike
   - thinking before doing; e.g., how to organize your bedroom, books, clothes, etc.

## Using Graphic Organizers

The concept of using graphic organizers is not new, but I have included it as a gentle reminder of just how many ways are available to present material graphically. As you know, a graphic organizer is a visual display that clearly shows relationships between fact, ideas, characters, systems, skills, etc. These visual aids appeal to all students, but especially to the visual learners. By teaching students when, where, and how to use graphic organizers, you are giving them skills for life. There are thousands of sites online that provide more information on graphic organizers than you will ever need, but do look there for additional help if necessary. Keep in mind that one of the objectives of this book is to simplify your job, and remove inefficient time stealers (such as web browsing) from it, so I've limited this section to a few of the most popular organizers.

### Tips for Using Any Graphic Organizer

Here are a few ideas to help students (and you) make the most of *any* graphic organizer you choose to use.

- Start small and simple; e.g., a family tree, the connection between two characters in a story.
- Provide a template, an outline for students to simply fill in for the first few experiences. There are free printable organizers on line, many of which are excellent.
- Help students pick out only the most important parts/ideas/components/etc. for their finished products.
- Model the creation of an organizer, and create and fill in one together, before sending them off on their own. Look at some completed organizers and discuss them in detail. (I cannot stress this modeling stage enough.)
- Use the SPARK teachable-moment procedure (see page 20) to incorporate graphic organizers at any time in content learning that lends itself to this strategy. In other words, be open to suggesting to students how often a graphic organizer can facilitate understanding, and how many different ways there are to do this.
- Present good organizers so that others can see and appreciate them. A Graphic Organizer Display Board is a highly visual presentation of different organizers, and can be changed regularly to maintain interest. Students learn from seeing what peers have done.
- Get into the habit of simply pointing out when/where a graphic organizer might be of benefit to students. During an art class where mixed media were being experimented with, the teacher pointed out casually that a graphic organizer would help to show how the media interacted. The next day a young man arrived at school with an amazing concept map that illustrated in color exactly what he had been doing in the art class. Although his art project was not great, his graphic organizer was!
- Once students are familiar with a variety of organizers, let them choose the organizer that they feel fits their particular situation best, rather than insisting that everyone use the same one.

## Venn Diagrams

Use primary colors for the circles; where they overlap use the secondary color created by the two primaries. The printing inside each part should match the circle colors.

Each circle represents all the elements of a set, and the overlapping section represents criteria relevant to both (or all) sets. This is one of the simplest graphic organizers, and one students quickly catch on to and enjoy using. See page 86 for a Venn Diagram Template.

## KWL Charts

These are simple representations of What I **K**now, What I **W**ant to Know, and What I **L**earned. A page is divided vertically into three parts, with the headings at the top of each section. I think we sometimes forget to use these uncomplicated charts, as they may seem unimportant, and yet they stimulate students to think ahead and then check and verbalize their thoughts. Non-writers can do beautiful KWL charts with illustrations. In fact, proficient writers can also make their KWLs more interesting with the addition of small illustrations. See page 87 for a KWL Chart Template.

## T-Charts

Make use of the three simplest graphic organizers (Venn, T-chart, KWL) as often as possible, spontaneously. For example, when reading a story, stop and compare two characters using a Venn; when doing a math problem, stop and T-chart possible solutions. In this way you teach students the usefulness of graphic organizers.

These straightforward two-part charts allow students to visually make comparisons. The Pro/Con chart is a perfect example, and one that we use consistently in our lives. A page is divided vertically into halves, with a heading at the top of each. Points are listed under each heading, offering a quick comparison of the two sides. Comparisons might include likes/dislikes, advantages/disadvantages, facts/opinions, and past/present—any two opposing conditions can be visually compared. This is another excellent tool to give students, not just for school, but for life. See page 88 for a T-Chart Template.

## Concept Maps

These are visual representations of how items/names/components/etc. are connected. They are usually hierarchical structures, beginning with the most important or broadest concepts, then breaking down to gradually smaller and more-detailed concepts or components. Sometimes these are referred to as trees, as the final structures resemble trees. The familiar family tree is a good example. The map basically shows how a main idea can be broken down into many related topics.

1. Help students determine a main idea, key question, salient theme, or belief.
2. Brainstorm as many related ideas, components, or subpoints as possible, making quick jot notes of them.
3. Rank all the subpoints according to relevance, with the most specific or smallest being last.
4. Join the components, moving from general to specific, or big to small.
5. Connect the points laterally and vertically, ending up with the most specific at the bottom.

## Webs

These are the simplest of the graphic organizers and can yet be effective with all ages. They basically begin with a basic idea or concept, then branch out to show connecting and relating points. Most frequently, the key point is in the centre of the page (usually contained in a circle, square, or oval) with lines radiating from this to attached other ideas or concepts. Young students can create webs with illustrations alone.

1. Show an example and discuss.
2. Discuss the main idea or concept that will go in the middle/top/side.
3. Brainstorm a few ideas for other relating concepts, then allow students to continue to generate the rest of them on their own.

## Mind Maps

These are exactly what the name suggests: visual diagrams depicting brainstorming in an organized yet nonlinear layout; i.e., organizing the results of brainstorming into manageable visual representation. A central or main topic or idea is shown in the middle, with as many lines radiating from it as necessary, then with additional lines radiating to related concepts from these. Bubbles or squares are situated at the ends of each radiating line. As a rule, most mind maps limit lines coming from the center to 4, with 2 lines coming from each subconcept. That's a total of 12 points or ideas generated from the main concept and grouped by subconcept. See page 89 for a 12-Point Mind Map Template.

**Mind maps are great for working through emotion-charged school situations that involve strong feelings; e.g., how to handle a bullying situation.**

1. Start with a problem or situation that requires a solution.
2. Share an example of a mind map and discuss, drawing attention to how the organizer can help to clarify thoughts and feelings.
3. Have students work in pairs to brainstorm the topic.
4. Students work individually using a teacher-provided template or creating their own as they work.
5. Debrief by discussing how the mind map helped with understanding of the topic, and of where else in life such a graphic organizer could be used.

## Student-Created Graphic Organizer

Once students are familiar with graphic organizers, they can create their own for specific situations. A Grade 3 student created the sample organizer when planning her birthday party. She brainstormed a to-do list, then created an organizer that allowed her to check off tasks as they were complete.

| What will I do to get ready? | ____ buy party favors & piñata |
| | ____ send out invitations |
| | ____ decorate & make cake |
| | ____ get a party dress |
| | ____ decorate my house |
| | ____ make grab bags |
| | ____ ask Nana to make a treasure hunt |
| What will happen at the party? | ____ play hide and seek in the yard |
| | ____ break the piñata |
| | ____ have a treasure hunt |
| | ____ open gifts |
| | ____ eat |
| What will happen after? | ____ say good bye and thank you |
| | ____ help mom clean up |

_____ write thank you notes
_____ sleep

Helping students create usable graphic organizers:

1. Remind students of previously used organizers.
2. Explain that you want them to think of a personal situation that they want to organize; e.g., homework, visit to relatives, report making.
3. Begin by giving them time to brainstorm everything related to the main topic.
4. Provide blank paper and encourage experimentation: *Where will you put your main idea? How many smaller ideas will you need? What design looks best to you?*
5. Remind them they can use any organizer they are aware of and/or combine components of several and/or create a new one perfect for what their own needs.
6. Present and discuss. Be enthusiastic about their use of these effective tools.

## Practice

It may seem flippant to include this as an everyday strategy but, in fact, it really *is* a strategy, and unfortunately we sometimes forget its importance. While research hasn't proven that practice makes perfect, it has shown that practice does, indeed, improve whatever is being rehearsed. And there is an art to practicing. You probably know people who can sit down and study and memorize, with no difficulty at all, while others have considerable trouble with the very same material. Where do you stand on this continuum? Consider the dancer who practices hours every day, or the athlete who works at his skills as a full-time job. Now think of a particular student you have, or had, who simply can't seem to retain anything and refuses to practice. Practicing is a skill. And skills can be trained. You are a teacher who can incorporate the strategy of practicing into your classroom agenda, and help your students not just with today's curriculum, but with their tomorrow lives.

1. Discuss the importance of practicing. If possible, use specific students' names as positive examples; e.g., "We know Roberto practices a lot to play the piano, because he is very good at it."
2. Draw parallels between practicing music, dance, sports, etc. and practicing school work.
3. Use a specific piece to be learned, practiced, understood, or even memorized: a poem, a math or science process; directions to do something; a literacy activity, such as practicing sentence writing.
4. Summarize the skill verbally and concisely. For example, "We all need to learn how to write a descriptive sentence by using action words and picture words."
5. Tell students exactly what they are going to do to practice this skill. For example, "To practice doing this, we are all going to write three good sentences about this picture. By writing three different sentences, we will be practicing descriptive writing."
6. For the whole class, teach/reinforce and always follow the steps for better practicing.

1. Create the right atmosphere; e.g., sit quietly at desk, possibly dim the lights, make sure you have everything you need; tell others not to bother you; turn off TV, music, phone, devices.

**How-to-Wow Practicing**
- Create atmosphere.
- Set your mood.
- Establish a goal.
- Be realistic (know yourself).
- Set breaks.
- Understand roadblocks.

2. Set your mood. Let's face it, no one really likes to practice, but facing it with a sour mood makes for wasted time. The advice to "Fake it till you make it" comes to mind. Fake feeling positive about the upcoming practice session. It is for *you*! *You* are the one who will benefit from it! *You* are in control! Remind yourself of how good you'll feel when you have completed the practice session, and how guilty you'll feel if you skip it or undermine its importance by fuming through it. Think about doing something you love to do. How do you feel at that time? Now compare that to how you feel doing the opposite. These positive and negative feelings have a huge impact on how well anything is accomplished, and it is a good idea to teach students how to identify and deal more effectively with their feelings about work/practice:

   - Use personal statements to open a discussion about how feelings affect work. Say something like, " I love _____, and feel excited and happy when I am doing that. But I don't like _____, and feel annoyed and upset when I have to."
   - Explain the connection between how we feel about something and how that affects work and/or practice.
   - Have students make a T-chart with the headings *Like* and *Dislike*. Have them jot down feeling words in the correct columns, and discuss with partners. (See page 88 for a T-Chart Template.)
   - Ask students how they might move some of the negative feelings to the Like list. Tell students that sometimes just faking feeling better about something, will actually help them to see it more positively.
   - Have them practice the Stop Sign technique: in their minds, they visualize a STOP sign whenever they start to experience a negative feeling, and then substitute a green light and a single positive phrase. For example, "When sitting down to do homework and feeling annoyed, STOP the feeling, and instead say to yourself, 'But I'll get a good mark, and mom will be proud.'"
   - Close by sharing that negative feelings are okay, as long as they don't interfere with what has to be done. And if we can identify them, we can replace them with more positive feelings that will not only make practice/work time easier, but also more productive.

3. Set a goal. Know exactly what you are attempting to accomplish, whether it's a dance or musical instrument practice, or a literacy reading or writing practice, or mathematical concepts practice. For example, learn or do this in/for 10 minutes or, say, until you have three good sentences. If what you are trying to do is big, break it into smaller units or components. For example, memorize this poem two lines at a time; write one sentence, reread it, make it better, then take a 30-second break

4. Be realistic. Know yourself. If you are a restless person, and what you are practicing will take longer than a few minutes, plan for shorter duration and more breaks. It is a good idea to help students appreciate their own limitations. They are at the stage where they are learning about themselves. What better time than now to help them understand their own degree of restlessness and/or focus?

- In minilesson format, discuss focus and restlessness. Use personal examples; e.g., "When I am doing something I like, such as ____, I can concentrate for a long time, but when I have to do _____, I find it hard to concentrate. Everyone is like that." Have them identify something they like to do and something they don't like to do, and mentally compare how well they focus and attend in each situation.
- Have them discuss in pairs each situation.
- Discuss ways to stay focused. Students often have their own ideas about this they can share. Close and summarize by reminding students that they are in control, and they can stay focused if they make up their minds to do so.

5. Discuss inserting breaks into a practice session. How many breaks? How often? The idea is to make students more aware of their own limitations, and to give them tools to more effectively deal with practice sessions. Following a talk about restlessness and focus, it makes sense to talk about breaks. The number of breaks and length of time between breaks will vary from student to student. Your job is to help individuals identify their own personal needs in this area. Because you know your students, you should be able to gently point them in the right direction. For example, one easily distracted young man felt he could practice in 30-minute chunks; his wise teacher managed to persuade him to work on 5-minute chunks to begin with, and they worked well for him.

6. Identify possible roadblocks and pitfalls before you begin. For example, if you think a friend is going to call, remove your phone for the duration of the practice period. If you expect to be hungry, eat something small before you begin. Also make sure you have absolutely everything you might need before you start.

7. Reward yourself. It is important to acknowledge even small practice and/or work sessions. One student places her tablet within view, as she knows she is allowed free screen time when she has completed her set study/practice/work time. So, once finished, acknowledge what you have done. Record it. Pat yourself on the back. Enjoy a different activity for a while.

Invite students to debate the expression *Practice makes perfect*. They can use a T-chart (Pro and Con) to organize thoughts, and then write or illustrate their own interpretation. See page 88 for a T-Chart Template.

## Tried and True Strategies

### Think–Pair–Share

This is not a novel idea, but one that has been in teachers' repertoires for years. However, it is so useful I include it here. It incorporates the important quality of sharing. For some students, it takes a lot of courage to share with others, even if that sharing is of knowledge. Think–Pair–Share not only expands wisdom, it offers practice in gentle sharing.

1. Have students individually think about a teacher-provided topic or question.
2. Pair students to discuss their various thoughts and decisions. Quiet talk is encouraged.
3. Encourage pairs to combine their thoughts into one cohesive presentation. This might be a single sentence, an illustration, a paragraph, a graphic organizer, etc.
4. Invite each pair to share with the rest of the class.
5. Debrief.

## Goal-Setting

"Setting goals is the first step in turning the invisible into the visible." — Tony Robbins

Students, sometimes with parents, sometimes with the teacher, sometimes on their own, set goals for themselves. This reflective activity requires students to self-evaluate; therefore, younger students require guidance. They need to identify areas of personal need or weakness, and for some students this is difficult, but once the idea has been introduced, they seem well able to run with it.

1. Teach minilessons on how to set realistic goals.
2. Do a model run with them. Invent a character who displays both strengths and weaknesses. As a class, set realistic goals for him.
3. Provide a goal-setting worksheet or notebook and allow regular time for personal goal-setting and evaluating.
4. Help students formulate plans of attack. What step(s) can they take to reach these goals? Have a class lesson on *How to reach your goal*. It is important that students understand the difference between realistic and unrealistic goals. A humorous minilesson about the setting of completely unrealistic goals (e.g., *I want to develop super powers*) might be beneficial.
5. If parents were not involved in the goal-setting, share the goals and the attack plans at a parent/teacher conference, or have students take their goal books/sheets home to be initialed by parents. Keep parents involved.
6. At regular intervals, take time to analyze student goals to see if they have been met. If they have not, try to help students figure out why and plan a new attack. If the goal is not meet, specifically teach how to adjust the steps taken to reach a goal. It is not necessary to change the goal, just the action plan.
7. Intermittently debrief the value of students' goal-setting and goal-evaluating experiences.

Share a personal goal (be sure it is not too personal; a silly goal works well) as well as your plans for reaching it. This modeling activity is motivating to all students.

## Talk to Teach

With permission from the principal, allow students to teach short lessons over the intercom at a specific time. They will present a couple of sentences (vetted by you, of course) to the school body as a leaning experience. The boy who brought the WW2 artifact gave a poignant 30-second talk about the ravages of war.

The familiar show-and-tell continues to be a very effective teaching strategy, but it is associated with younger students; consequently older students don't want to be involved in it at all. So welcome to Talk to Teach! This is essentially the same strategy with a different name, but it works with students of all ages. A student-presented item is discussed, offering many literacy development strategies. The way in which Talk to Teach differs from show-and-tell is that students are asked to bring an item that they can use to teach something to the rest of the class. For example, a Grade 6 boy brought a WW2 artifact on loan from his grandfather, and taught the class interesting facts about that time in history. A word of caution: Always check to see what object the student plans to share before giving them the floor. A very embarrassed young teacher shared with me how one of her students brought a condom (in its wrapper) as a show-and-tell item, and although she caught it before it became a class topic of interest, he had already shared it with several peers.

## Learning Centres

Learning centres are not the same as learning stations. Learning stations work in sequence or progression with each other. Learning centres work in isolation.

I have included this familiar strategy as an everyday strategy because it is used primarily to supplement other methods of teaching. A note needs to be added here to distinguish between learning centres and learning stations. Stations are connected; they work in sequence or progression with each other. Centres work in isolation. Although centres are used primarily in early grades, they are equally effective at all grades if the materials provided allow students to work at many levels. In fact, older students, right up to high school, enjoy the challenge offered by creative in-class centres.

Centres can do anything you want them to—challenge students in science, give them extra practice in math, etc. There is a misconception that centre creation is extremely time-consuming. It doesn't have to be. All it really requires is your goal (what do you want the centre to do), a little creativity, and about a half hour of your time. I know one lucky teacher who simply lets her parent volunteer know the objective for a centre and the parent creates it. We can't all be so lucky, but we can set up a centre in a short time and it can exist as is for several weeks. Then, it may need only minor housekeeping in the form of new materials to keep it vibrant.

**Set up a single learning centre as a reward for students who have completed work or in some way earned the right to use it. In it, have materials that are interesting and motivating, such as puzzles, games, or tech devices.**

1. Set up a centre with a specific goal in mind.
2. Make sure everything required for the activities at the centre are there.
3. Post a list of centre directions, or walk non-readers through it.
4. Take a few minutes of class time to discuss the use and expectations of the centre.
5. How and when you use them is entirely up to you, but it is a good idea have a timer at the centre so that no student remains there too long.

## The Wow of Literacy Strategies

When a teacher teaches a student to read, the teacher has given that child a super power. What could possibly have a greater wow factor than that? All teachers have witnessed the proverbial light going on, the "aha!" moment when a student finally gets it. This is a huge wow, experienced by the student and witnessed by the teacher. When a struggling student reaches this wonderful point in literacy development, the wow is almost overwhelming. I witnessed a reluctant reader, a Grade 2 student, pick up a graphic novel and read on her own for the first time. She literally glowed with pride. Yes, many of the words were substitutions, but she got the gist and she was reading. What a wow for all concerned!

There are so many strategies for teaching literacy that I have decided to present only those I feel are the most effective and most consistently used. You will already be familiar with them, but perhaps not how to make them really productive.

### Beginning Reading

Beginning readers come in many sizes and shapes, with as wide a range of abilities as you can possibly imagine. For this reason, teaching beginning readers can be extremely difficult. The basic strategies for these students include phonics, fluency, comprehension, and vocabulary.

### Phonics

Phonics is the learn-to-read method of linking sounds together in order to make words. Teachers are very aware of the benefits of phonics in the early years of reading, but a brief review might be helpful here.

1. Follow the steps of phonics instruction (initial consonant sounds, short vowels, two-letter blends, three-letter blends, endings). These are clearly delineated in teachers' manuals, reading and phonics series, and online, so this is the only reference that will be made to the sequence of phonic instruction. Just remember that the established sequence is one that has been proven to work; avoid changing it.

2. Use a context approach. Point out phonemes you have covered in class in text everywhere and all the time. For example, after learning about homophones, the wise teacher pointed out *write* and *right* on a sign posted in the school hall that read, *Write your name in the right column please.*

3. Play phonics games.

4. Use as many "tricks" as possible. These may seem silly to you, but to children who are struggling, they can be life savers. Here are a few:

   - For *b* and *d* confusion, draw a shape around the word *bed*. The shape looks like a bed. Once students see that, they more easily remember that the curve of the *b* at the head of the bed turns toward the middle of the bed, while the curve of the *d* at the end also turns to the middle.

   - For upper case *B* and lower case *b*, teach *Bees all fly in the same direction*; i.e., the curves of both small *b* and capital *B* turn the same way.

   - For upper case *D* and lower case *d*, teach *Big daddy* D *faces his son little* d.

   - For two vowels together teach, *When two vowels go walking, the first does the talking*; i.e., *ea* says long *e*.

   - For the silent *e* and previous vowel being long rule, teach *With* e *on the end, the first vowel's a friend. And friends tell their names.*

5. Read and write everyday.

## Phonics Games

### FIND THAT SOUND

Students move around the room trying to be the first to touch objects that start (or end) with a specific sound.

### WHERE IN THAT SONG

Play a popular tune and have students attempt to identify words with specific beginning/ending sounds

### JOIN WITH ME

Half the class is given cue cards with word endings (e.g., *-at, -an, -up*) and the other half has cards with initial consonants. Students mingle, match up with each other to make words, and record the words in printing. At the end of a set time, the students with the most correct words are the winners (of course, you can skip having a winner if you wish).

### CLAP THE SOUND

As a class, listen to a piece of content text, a story, or a poem. Every time students hear a specific sound, they clap once. To make this more difficult, add a double clap for a second sound. You can make this a team challenge by awarding a point to the team that claps first, and subtracting a point if an incorrect clap is made.

**How-to-Wow Phonics**
- Use established phonic rules and sequences of instruction.
- Teach in context.
- Play phonics games.
- Use "tricks."
- Read/write daily.

### SOUNDS ON ME

This game requires students to identify specific phonemes on themselves. This time you tell them what phoneme you are looking for. For example if you say "Short *e*," students should point to a leg or their neck. Once they have correctly identified the body part, they write that word on a provided handout. A good follow up is to provide an outline of a figure (you could trace a gingerbread-person cookie cutter), and have students print the found body parts in the right places. You can also make this a competitive game by having teams play against each other; the first team to identify the body part gets a point.

### CUT AND PASTE SCAVENGER HUNT

You know how much young students love to cut and paste. This game capitalizes on that and reinforces learned phonics rules and awareness of phonemes. Provide pieces of newspapers and/or magazines, scissors, glue, and cue sheets for each individual or for pairs. The cue sheets have boxes with headings that list exactly what you want students to find. For example, boxes might include *blends, short vowels, long vowels, silent* e, *pronouns, contractions, plurals*. The words being scavenged can be whatever relates to what you have been teaching in class. This is an excellent reviewing and reinforcing activity, and students thoroughly enjoy it. You can make it a competition by having pairs race against each other; the first pair to find the required number of words and correctly glued them to their chart wins.

### WORD FAMILY FEUD

This game can be highly competitive or merely fun. Word families can be based on the word head, also known as the base, stem, or root (e.g., *play* is the word head for *player, playing, playful, playpen*), or a specific phonetic component, such as the *ck* blend. You will make this decision based on what you have been covering in class and what you see your students need help with. You will need to create word-family cards. Use blank index cards, cut up construction paper, or purchase blank flash cards. On one side print the word families you want to reinforce.

1. Divide the class into teams of 5–6 players.
2. Explain the game goal: to make as many word families within a time limit as you can.
3. Model: randomly choose a card and, as a class, create as many words as possible that fit into that family.
4. Have students take turns selecting a card, then allow about 2 minutes for teams to jot down as many words as they can.
5. Call, "Stop! Pencils down."
6. Draw another card and repeat. An alternative way to choose a card is to have teams take turns rolling a small pebble on a table where the family cards are spread face-down. Where the pebble rests, that card is turned over and the race begins.

## Fluency

The ability to read smoothly and with expression is referred to as reading fluency. Beginning readers are so concerned with getting the words correct, they often completely miss what they are reading. Their reading becomes choppy and slow, and they get little or no enjoyment from it. As teachers, we must always keep in mind that books are portable magic, and that learning to read and enjoy that magic is the goal we have for all our students. Helping them read fluently, with passion and excitement, is a hugely important step in that process. It is possible to encourage and reinforce fluency even at early reading levels.

1. Model fluent reading. Read often, with lots of expression, and passion and excitement. Your voice is your tool; use it powerfully.

2. Read together. Provide a single sentence that lends itself to lots of expression, such as *The girl was tiptoeing through the dark woods when a huge spider dropped on her head.* Read this together several times, then have students practice it on their own. Finally share the sentence readings and discuss who had the most expression. The rereading as a class allows a degree of memorization of the sentence, so that even reluctant readers can read it.

3. Shared reading: You read a line or section, then the student reads a line or section. Shared reading can also be done with peers. Pair a strong student with a weaker one, but keep changing partners so that feelings don't get hurt.

4. Provide many opportunities for rereading. Help students to plow through a book the first time or first few times, have them read to a buddy or volunteer, and have them read to you before asking them to read it aloud in class.

5. Use the rebus approach, in which small illustrations are drawn by the student adjacent to any word they are having trouble with on a first or second reading. If the student can see the picture and not have to struggle with a word, reading automatically becomes more fluent. Of course this only works on text that students are allowed to write on, but the illustrations can be small pencil drawings, easily erased later. The illustrations do not have to be literal depictions of the word; they can be whatever reminds the student of the word itself. For example, a Grade 1 student was having difficulty with the word *excitement*, and even with repeated readings she was forgetting it. She drew a small star that looked like fireworks over the word, explaining that she felt excitement when she saw fireworks, and she never missed the word again. Shortly after that, the teacher noticed that the student was recognizing *excitement* in other texts where no fireworks had been drawn.

6. Use the Buddy Read system. Older students are paired with younger ones to both read to them and listen to them read. This is advantageous to both parties and gives the younger ones another example of fluent reading. If you can set up with another class to have regular Buddy Reads, try to stick to the established schedule so that all students have this time to look forward to. I have witnessed Buddy Reads where the two buddies were given 15 minutes of together time anywhere in the school to sit quietly and read, and pairs literally disappeared into corners, hallways, and under desks, then reappeared when the 15 minutes were up. Both partners kept a Buddy Read journal. Younger students printed words or drew illustrations, or asked questions. Older students kept a record of how well their buddies were doing, of any positive changes they witnessed, of any difficulties they or their buddies were having. In both cases, the journals were informative and useful to teachers for planning future minilessons. The younger students felt important when buddied with older students. The older students enjoyed their teacher roles and felt that what they were doing was meaningful.

7. Allow ample practice time for oral reading, with partners, volunteers, or buddies. If you want a student to read out loud in front of peers, give them the material well ahead of time, encourage practicing both at home and at school,

**Giving lots of time for children to practice new skills progressively is what defines good teaching.**

then use your instincts to determine if they are confident enough to do this task without anxiety. A poor reader who struggles and stammers in front of peers will suffer more than just from reading reluctance. Every oral reading experience must be a positive one.

8. Sing/Read. Model singing a section to be read. Use a familiar tune, or make one up. For example, to the tune of the alphabet song, sing/read the sentence, "The cat ran home to get a drink. He met a dog on the way there." You might need to force the words to the existing melody. The act of putting the words to music relieves some of the tension students may have about reading, and allows them the freedom to read (sing) more fluently. Have students sing/read to each other. Any students who want to share should be allowed to, but keep this voluntary.

## Fluency Games

Although not games in the truest sense of the word, these fluency-enhancing activities are fun for students and can easily be introduced as games.

### ROBOT READ

Model reading like a robot, slowly and without expression, deliberately pausing after each word. Invite students to do the same. This gives them permission to read without fluency while they are learning.

### PUPPET/DOLL/FIGURINE READ

Like the Robot Read, this strategy takes anxiety about oral reading from the child and puts it on whatever object they have chosen to be their voice. With the puppet/doll/figurine/stuffy in hand, ventriloquist style, the student reads a short practice selection. Model this strategy first with your own object; I once witnessed a smart teacher grab a pencil from her desk and speak the reading through the pencil. Start by allowing the object to introduce itself: "Hi. My name is Mr. Pencil and I'm going to read to you from this book." Then read, using the voice of the object whenever possible. For time efficiency you can do this as a small-group activity, where each object reads to 4 or 5 other objects within the group.

### RHYME READ

Choose short interesting rhymes. Read the rhyme *to* the students, then *with* the students. Then have students orally identify the rhyming sounds, followed by highlighting or circling the rhyming parts of all the words that rhyme. You can follow up by having pairs write more lines to the poems, or having individuals illustrate the poems. You can make this competitive by dividing the class into groups, giving each group a few written rhymes, providing the general directions, then allowing a set time (5 minutes) for finding and writing the rhyming words. Once they have found all the words hidden in the poems, have them try to lengthen the list with as many other words fitting the rhyme family as they can. The team with the most correct words wins. Here are some samples of short rhyming poems:

I eat my peas with honey.
I've done it all my life.

"Reading should not be presented to children as a chore or duty. It should be offered to them as a precious gift." — Kate DiCamillo. The more enthusiastic, engaged, and excited you are when you read to or with students, the more they will try to emulate this stance in their own reading.

It makes the peas taste funny
But it keeps them on my knife.
— Anonymous

There was a wise owl who lived in an oak.
The more he heard, the less he spoke,
The less he spoke the more heard.
Why aren't we all like that wise old bird?
— Anonymous

Jake the snake wanted to bake.
A beautiful cake he wanted to make.
Jake ate the cake beside the lake
And slithered home with a bellyache.
— Anonymous

## Comprehension

**How-to-Wow Comprehension**
- Prepare
- Explain/Model/Guided Practice/ Application
- Encourage checking for understanding
- Play comprehension games

Comprehension is the understanding of the meaning of what is read. Have you ever been reading a book or magazine when you suddenly realize you have no idea what you've just read? It happens to all of us, but as educated adults we can usually figure out why we are not comprehending, why the words are just words with no attached meaning. Students who have difficulties with comprehension are not so lucky. Sometimes they can be beautiful, fluent readers, but when asked a simple comprehension question, they have no idea what they just read. That teachers can provide effective teaching strategies for improving students' comprehension is a proven fact. The four steps to doing this are worthy of review before a more-in depth examination of additional tips and techniques.

1. Explain. Teach/talk specifically about understanding what we are reading. Then introduce a strategy (or several, depending on the ages/needs of students) by saying its name (e.g., This is called identifying the problem) and clearly explaining how it will help them to comprehend. Tell them it is necessary for them to ask questions of themselves while reading.
2. Model the strategy. Read a paragraph. Stop. "I don't get what the author means by 'winning was actually losing to John'. I have identified the problem, now how do I solve it?"
3. Using guided practice, show students how to take the three steps to better understanding:

    Step 1.  Restate the sentence that is troublesome in different words. "So if John wins, he must lose something?"
    Step 2.  Look back. "What is there in the text before this that might help me understand?" Reread a part explaining that if John won, his best friend would lose.
    Step 3.  Look ahead. The next chapter is called John Loses—on Purpose.

4. Summarize findings. Using the example in step 3: "So I think the author means that if John wins, he will lose his best friend. So maybe he doesn't want to win."
5. Have students demonstrate application of this strategy by following the same steps on with a different text.

## Quick Comprehension Strategies

### THINK-ALOUDS

Read a small section to students, then stop and describe what internal strategies you are using to determine meaning. For example, say "I can see this beach scene in my mind and I think there might be a dangerous wave coming. I can tell this from the words..." Use the words "Think out loud" to explain to students what you are doing. In pairs have students "think out loud" about a short paragraph or piece of text.

### SELF-QUESTIONING

The example on page shows this type of effective comprehension process. Teach as many strategies as possible during a class reading, not in isolation. Strategies include:

- Asking self-questions: *What is this about?*
- Identifying uncertainties: *What don't I understand?*
- Identifying important points: *Why is this sentence/paragraph/section important?*
- Identifying author's purpose: *What does the author want me to know?*

Specifically teach about the four types of answers to self-questions:

1. Right there: answers are directly in text or picture
2. Think and search: answers are in the text but are located in more than one place
3. Already known: answers are based on what students already know from the text or can surmise from the reading
4. On your own: answers are based on prior knowledge and/or experience

## Lessons on Comprehension

### REASON FOR READING

Give students a reason for the reading before they begin. In other words, tell them what to read for; focus their attention before they read. Even if the text is a picture book, give a reason, such as "Read to find out what the character likes/does/sees/etc." If students are choosing their own resources, as when researching for a project or report, remind them to determine specific reasons for their readings: "Exactly what are you seeking?"

### EXISTING KNOWLEDGE

Tap into existing knowledge bases. Before students begin reading, have them reflect on what they already know about or related to the subject. If the reading is a narrative, ask them to recall what they know about setting, plot, climax, etc. This stimulating of knowledge bases helps with comprehension of new text.

### SUMMARIZE

Make summaries together for a variety of texts. Encourage the making of summaries at regular intervals when reading for fact or pleasure. Teach students that summarizing in their heads as they read will improve comprehension.

Have students generate questions for peers from the text, then share and answer these questions.

GRAPHIC ORGANIZERS

Use graphic organizers (see pages 86–89) to help students visualize what they are reading. Younger children can draw illustrations.

LOOK FOR CLUES

Teach students to look for clues everywhere: in titles, charts, pictures, index, glossary. Remind them every time they read to find the clues first.

## Comprehension Games

- Jeopardy-style Game: Provide an answer from the text and invite students to provide the possible question
- Mash-up Stories: Make copies of short stories, one copy per group or pair. Cut the story into as many parts as you want, mix them together, and attach them together with a paper clip. Students first read the story in their groups or pairs. Then they try to reassemble the story correctly without looking at the original. The first group to finish correctly wins. To add more challenge, throw in a sentence or two from a completely different story or text. If the students have comprehended correctly, they will quickly recognize the parts that do not belong.
- Big Ball Knows All: Inflate two or three plastic beach balls and cover them with strips of masking tape on which comprehension questions are written. The questions can vary in difficulty. The goal is to correctly answer whatever question the thumb is on when the ball is caught. In teams, toss the ball around and whoever catches it has to answer. A correct answer earns the team a point. No answer or incorrect answer equals 0 points, and the ball gets tossed again.
- Cloze It: Teams challenge each other to correctly fill in missing words/phrases from a previously read text or story. Write sentences on slips of paper, then place the slips face-down. Team members take turns picking a slip and reading it to the class, filling in the missing parts as they read. Sentences must be read fluently and without long pauses. A correctly read sentence earns the team a point. An example of a cloze sentence from the story Goldilocks and the Three Bears would be: "When _____ found the empty cottage she first saw the ____."
- True/False: A whole-class activity or a team game, the goal of True/False is to determine if the statement provided by you or a chosen narrator is true or false. Create a list of statements related to the text/narrative/poem/etc. read previously. You can simply read the statements and call for responses, or you can give the statements to a student narrator to read. You can use this as a whole-class activity, or have teams play against each other, answering in turn and gaining points for correct responses. If using this last method, you might want to put the statements on individual cards or paper slips and turn them face-down so that statements are given randomly. The statements should be of a wide variety, including direct recall, making of inferences or assumptions, predicting, summarizing, etc. For example, for Goldilocks and the Three Bears, you might say, "Goldilocks ate the little bowl of porridge, then went right to bed." This is false: she didn't go to bed; she sat on the three chairs. Students

"The more that you read, the more things you will know. The more you learn, the more places you'll go."
— Dr. Seuss.

must identify false statements and correct them. Students love this game and become experts at picking up the smallest falsehoods.

## Helping the Reluctant Reader

Some young students seem unmotivated or unable to grasp the concept of reading. These students cause considerable anxiety for teachers, and certainly there is little or no wow experienced by either student or teacher. But there are ways to help them.

1. Work with these students using short, fun, easy practice sessions, such as having them read to you from books that involve minimum difficulty for them.
2. Share short, amusing quotes like one from Dr Seuss: "The more you read, the more things you will know. The more things you know the more places you'll go." Have this quote visible and read it together often. It contains easy vocabulary and is a vivid reminder of the importance of learning to read.
3. Take some time to try to determine why the reader is reluctant. Is it a decoding problem? A motivational problem? A self-consciousness problem? If you can't figure it out from listening to them read, ask them outright why they dislike reading. Sometimes the direct approach is enlightening.
4. Provide extrinsic motivation (these students are not intrinsically motivated to read) such as tangible rewards for small accomplishments.
5. Have in-class read-for-fun periods, in which all students read whatever they like. No questions asked! Include materials such as magazines, graphic novels, comics, picture books, sales fliers, or chapter books from which students can choose. Emphasize choice!
6. Make a point of recognizing even small successes. Send notes home congratulating the student on achievements.
7. Use peers. Place students in groups of differing reading abilities and have them read to each other. Encourage turn-taking, but also allow students to pass if it is too uncomfortable for them to read aloud. The reluctant readers will still learn from their peers, even if they don't read aloud themselves.
8. Use fun activities like modified readers theater. Create your own drama with characters who speak (read) only words that are easy for the reluctant reader. Allow students to practice their parts before sharing.
9. Read! Read! Read to students from a wide variety of resources, and with enthusiasm and excitement. You can do this. You are a teacher and teachers are, after all, consummate actors!
10. Have daily times when everyone is required to do nothing but read. What they read is their choice, but for 10 minutes (or whatever works for you), reading is the only activity going on. Keep this consistent. You must read too. Students will quickly learn that at some specific time every day, they must read, so they will have material that is interesting to them. Have on hand a wide variety of reading materials. Some students may just picture read for that time, but that's okay. Noses in books—that's what it's all about.
11. Teach a specific lesson on the many values of reading. Sometimes reluctant readers do not see the benefits of doing something that is difficult for them.
12. Use technology to hook students into reading. There are many wonderful sites that encourage beginning readers and, since all kids love technology, use them as much as possible.

13. Have students of all ages do brief book talks about favorite books—even picture books. Model first by telling about your favorite book, then either draw names for random sharing or ask for volunteers, with the understanding that eventually every student will give a book talk.
14. Find high-interest/low-vocabulary books, available even at the early reader stage (although most of them are designed for older readers). There are even publishers that specialize in books for reluctant readers.

## Beginning Writing

### Printing

It is not within the scope of this book to deal with dysgraphia or dyspraxia, but only with the more-common problems of early writers.

Writing involves so much more than just learning to form the letters on a page, but that in itself can be a huge task. Teaching young students to print can be daunting; it is difficult for small fingers to create the perfect swirls and sticks. Of course, you begin with the alphabet (the familiar alphabet song) and air writing (tracing big letters in the air), using multisensory manipulative objects (letters in sand, clay, play dough, etc), and then finally copying individual letters on paper. Once students are printing, a number of common errors may appear, such as letter reversal or letters floating in the air. There are tricks and techniques to help reverse these errors.

- For *b/d* confusion, print the word *bed* and draw a line around it so that the figure resembles an actual bed. The *b* turns toward the middle of the bed as the pillow; the *d* turns toward the middle also, forming the foot of the bed. Once students see this, every time they come to the letters *b* or *d* they think of the bed.
- For letters with tails (*p, g, q, y*) that tend to float in the air with the tips of the tails on the line, use the cue, *Tails must stay under the table.* The line on which the students are printing is the table and, once they can see this, those tails stay where they belong.
- For lack of spaces between words, use the finger technique. Students put their finger after a word to mark the space before beginning the next word.
- For letters being spaced too far apart, teach *Letters of a word are a family, and they need to stay together.*
- For letters containing both a circle and a line: some students start with the circle then attach the line, making the final letter look clumsy. Teach, *The line is like a slide, and you always start at the top of a slide.* This encourages starting in the correct place for these types of letters.
- Practice! Practice! Practice! Once again, practice is the key. Keep encouraging those young writers by acknowledging small improvements and successes.

"Our greatest weakness lies in giving up. The most certain way to succeed is always to try just one more time." — Thomas Edison

### Spelling

Spelling is a necessary component of writing but, in the past, it has usually been taught in isolation. We know now that this is not the best approach. But that doesn't mean you need to give up the weekly spelling lists and quizzes that have been ingrained in teachers since the beginning of time. What it does mean is that you need to be aware of the limitations of isolated spelling words/lists, and to supplement them with other strategies.

One point to keep in mind is that most students do not love spelling lists, quizzes, tests. They do not see the merit in them. Do you? Of course you want those early phonetic spellers to learn the correct ways to spell. Of course you want your students to present as educated adults some day, adults with good spelling. Of course you know that texting, with all its totally phonetic spelling, plays havoc with "real" spelling. But what can you do?

To begin with, always point out the merits of good spelling. Draw attention to spelling words in text, on charts, in narratives—everywhere. And also draw attention to incorrect spelling in public places, such as the sign that read *Keep clam, and check your spelling.* Laugh with your students at mistakes such as these, and discuss the effect a mistake like this has on readers. Or share the true tale of a young man who was applying for a position as shop boy at a local mechanic's garage. He had a great résumé and was sure he'd get the job. However, the position went to a younger boy who had less experience. When the older boy asked the employer why he had been rejected, the man showed the boy the résumé he had submitted, pointing out several glaring spelling errors within the responses to questions. When the angry young man asked what spelling had to do with working on cars, the potential employer explained that his poor spelling was a reflection on him as a person. Spelling counts, and spell check is not always available nor reliable.

You are aware of the different ways to teach spelling that show up in teachers' guides, curriculum content, and, of course, online, so this book will not deal with that. Instead, I will try to offer a few different ideas. But first, a quick review. How does the busy teacher teach students to spell?

**Allow beginning spellers to spell phonetically; e.g., *lemn* for *lemon*. At this developmental stage, point out the correct spelling but avoid belaboring the point or you might discourage writing altogether.**

1. First and foremost, talk about the importance of having good spelling. Discus why it is necessary. Point out the difference between spelling while texting and spelling while writing. Remind students that texting is like having a conversation, while writing is a formal endeavor that requires attention to spelling.
2. Begin with phonics and phonetic awareness. The application of the phonetic spelling strategy gives students a good start.
3. Teach spelling rules in context. Such rules include when to use *k* and *c* (think "kid's club"), when to double an end consonant, how to make words plural, "*i* before *e*, except after *c*," etc. You can find all the spelling rules online if you need them.
4. Teach useful mnemonics. Here are a few good ones.

**The best mnemonics are the ones kids make up themselves. If particular words are troubling them, have them create their very own mnemonics.**

- A fri*end* is there till the *end*.
- An *e* at the end, tells the name of its friend; i.e., the *e* at the end of a word makes the previous vowel long, or say its name.
- To spell *necessary* say "Never eat cakes, eat salmon sandwiches and raspberry yogurt."

5. Break words into smaller, more-manageable parts. This is officially referred to as segmenting, but to students, it's "breaking them up." Make this into a game by giving pairs a list of multisyllable words they will find in a subject area or reader and having them work together to correctly segment them.
6. Talk about the *Does it look right?* strategy. If a word is spelled incorrectly, ask the student if it looks right to them. If they say yes (which is often the case), point out calmly that it doesn't look quite right to you and ask how it might be changed. This is the art of gently guiding instead of pounding facts in.

7. Make a game of your own mistakes. Tell the class you are going to write a message to them on the board or chart paper, then write a simple message in which several words are incorrectly spelled. They will delight in finding your errors and pointing them out to you. This is a genuine learning experience. A Grade 2 teacher wrote *tday we mite go two the jim to ply baskitbal*. Students loved it. Just be sure the note you write is relevant—something real and/or meaningful to the students.

8. Invite students to teach you. Collect common spelling errors from their written work and share the list, asking them to help you figure out what is wrong. It is interesting how they carry out the teaching part. One Grade 1 student, teaching the correct spelling of *Canada* (written *Canda*), said, "Say after me—there are three *a*'s in *Canada*." Then she went on, "Okay, so how many *a*'s in *Canada*?"

9. Use online spelling games sites. These are many and varied; all are excellent reinforcers of good spelling.

10. Play spelling games. Some familiar ones that encourage good spelling are Hangman, crosswords, word searches, and word scrambles (in which mixed-up letters need reorganizing to make words).

SPELLING GAMES

See page 41 for more spelling games.

- Yes, Yes, No!: Students pick a difficult word from their spelling list and write three statements about it, two true or *yes* statements, and one false or *no* statement. In pairs, small groups, or the whole class, other students try to identify the *no* statement. Encourage students to write statements that show they are really looking at the word in question. This intense consideration of a word by both the student writing the statements and other students is an excellent spelling strategy. An example for the word ambitious would be:

  1. This word is an adjective. (yes)
  2. The opposite of this word is *casual*. (yes)
  3. This word has the little word "bitious" in it. (no such little word)

- Word Chains: Have students connect all the words in their spelling list in some manner. Creative kids can sometimes get all the words to work in a single sentence. Others may need to add "helper words" (not on the original list) to make sentences. The goal is to link the words in meaningful sentences with the least number of helpers.

- Musical Words: Ask students to find tunes they can fit their spelling words into. They can force the words to fit the tune they select, as long as they can justify to you and the class why this works. In other words, for the Grade 1 spelling list *duck, muck, luck, cat, sat, fat, chin chick, chat*, a young student selected the tune "Five Little Ducks Went Swimming"; he changed the words to "Five little ducks swam into the muck, what bad luck, the fat cat said. Four little ducks stopped for a chat with a chick who sat in the muck." This was quite ingenious, but simple sentences explaining the connection would be enough.

- Picture the Words: Provide an ample supply of magazines, newspapers, sheets of small coloring figures, etc. Have students find pictures that somehow fit the spelling words and glue them beside the words. It's interesting how creative kids can be— one girl put an illustration of her teacher beside the word *marvelous*. This activity draws attention to words in ways other than simply memorizing the correct order of the letters.

## Grammar

"Readers make writers and writers make readers." — Carl Mckever

Is there really a place for good grammar these days? Absolutely! And if you are helping your students learn to use proper grammar in both oral and written language, you are doing them a great service. The English language is notoriously difficult to learn. Rather than considering the inductive vs deductive methods of teaching grammar, this book will take the stance that the best way to teach grammar is in context, in the meaningful and extensive reading and writing that goes on in class. Start with a few basic rules, then use literature to reinforce the concepts. Always keep in mind that lots and lots of reading and writing are the absolute best strategies for teaching good grammar, and that even grammar instruction can wow a class if handled with a dash of enthusiasm and pizzazz.

## Grammar Games

### MAD LIBS

See page 45 for more grammar games.

This is an old favorite that is well-suited for reinforcing grammar once the initial parts of speech have been learned. You simply write a sentence leaving out specific nouns, adjectives, verbs, and adverbs; you identify the parts of speech that should go in the blanks, for example:

_____(proper noun) was _____ (verb ending with -ing) at home when suddenly a _____ (noun) _____ (verb ending with -ed).

It's fun to have each student fill in the blanks and then compare the sometimes ridiculous results. Or you can have a partners challenge to see who can create the most interesting sentences. Or you can use actual student's names in the sentences to up the motivational factor:

Joe and Anna were _____(verb ending with -ing) and then _____(pronoun) _____(verb ending with -ed) _____(adverb).

This sort of personal approach really gets students involved, and you can easily see how this game reinforces parts of speech awareness.

### MATCH-UPS

You will need to have a set of cards (index cards, slips of paper) on which are written subjects and predicates. Some subjects will be plural, some singular. Then predicates will also be both singular and plural. In pairs, one person holds the subjects, while the other holds the predicates. They attempt to match up all their cards so that they have correct sentences. It is a good idea to have students create their own subject/predicate cards then match up with different students to make sentences. To increase the game aspect, make it competitive by having all pairs use the same subjects/predicates and the first pair to correctly match all of them up wins.

### AWESOME ADVERBS

Adverbs can be confusing, especially the ones that do not end in *ly*. Create a large stack of adverb cards, being sure to include more difficult adverbs, such as *almost, very, too, enough*, etc. Have students take turns saying sentences about anything (you can use sentence starter pictures if you want to), randomly selecting an adverb card, then re-saying their sentence so that it includes the adverb. This can be done as an individual activity by displaying some adverb cards and having students write their own sentences.

### CROSS TWO

Create a regular crossword puzzle using only grammar terms; e.g., *noun, preposition*, etc. Or bump up the intensity by creating a crossword that indicates which part of speech a word must be to fit the boxes. For this game, give students any two grammar terms; they have to choose words that not only fit the terms, but cross each other, as in a crossword. For example if your terms are *noun* and *verb*, the student could write

S<br>M A N<br>T

*Man* is the noun and *sat* the verb that crosses it. It is easy to see how Cross Two can facilitate the awareness of parts of speech.

### PREPOSITION WHO-DONE-IT?

As you know, if prepositions are not used properly, their antecedents can be unclear and confusing. For example: "The children planted the seeds. *They* were excited." Who was excited? The children? The seeds? This conundrum makes for a fun pairs game in which students must decide, between provided nouns and/or proper nouns, who actually "dun-it." Each partner chooses a different noun in the sentence and tries to convince the other that they are right. Obviously there is no right or wrong answer, as either noun could be the antecedent, but the challenge comes with the student's ability to support their claim.

> Sample Sentence: The ball hit the bat with a loud crack. *It sailed off right toward the pitcher.*
> Student A: I chose the ball. *The ball flew toward the pitcher, who caught it and got the batter out.*
> Student B: I chose the bat. *After the hit, the bat flew out of the batter's hands and hit the pitcher on his head.*

You can see how students need to recognize the nouns, understand antecedents, then create interesting sentences. This is grammar in context. If you want to up the gaming aspect, have a jury whose job it is to choose the best sentence.

### PARTS OF SPEECH MAZE

This is usually an individual activity, but can work with pairs, where different pairs compare completed work. The game requires a basic knowledge of parts of speech and a curious mind. Students are given pages with several sentences written on them. Their first job is to identify every part of speech you request from a list on the board. If you have covered only nouns and verbs, your list will include only those two. The more parts of speech your students are aware of, the longer this list. Once the parts of speech have been found and underlined, students replace each with a different word that is the same part of speech; for example:

Based on the game Candy Land, the Grammar Land downloadable game board provides a fun way for pairs to work on grammar concepts. A game for two players, it can be used for reinforcement or in a centre.

A dog walked slowly toward the big, old tree.

Students identify nouns, verbs, adverbs, adjectives, prepositions: A <u>dog</u> (noun) <u>walked</u> (verb) <u>slowly</u> (adverb) <u>toward</u> (preposition) the <u>big (adjective)</u>, <u>old (adjective)</u> <u>tree</u> (noun).

Student wrote: A pug jumped nervously away from an ugly, bent plant.

## PARLEY TO IMPRESS

This activity is a perfect way for students to practice good grammar in oral communication.

1. Prepare a list of common incorrect grammar verbalization. Here are a few examples:

   > I seen
   > I done
   > I don't got no
   > I gots
   > He ain't

2. Open a discussion using obviously poor grammar and see if, or how many, students catch it; for example: "So, yesterday we done some grammar, but I don't got no idea if you really understand because I ain't seen your journals yet." This sentence is so glaringly bad, it is hard to even write it!
3. If students don't react immediately, ask if what you said sounded right to them, and repeat it if necessary.
4. Lead the discussion toward the use of good grammar in speech.
5. Bring up the idea of slang vs proper talk. When is each appropriate? Help students come to understand that in most situations, school especially, proper talk is better talk. Texting talk can be compared to slang talk; i.e., okay between friends and in casual situations.
6. Pair up students and provide a copy of the incorrect phrases to each pair.
7. One student uses an incorrect phrase in a conversation, while the partner corrects it. Have students keep switching positions.
8. Circulate to be sure students are fixing the mistakes appropriately, and watch for a few really good pairs who can share with the entire class.
9. Close by reminding students to be on the lookout for these specific grammar errors and to correct them in their own minds if/when they hear them.

> "Your grammar is a reflection of your image. Good or bad, you have made an impression and, like all impressions, you are in total control." — Jeffrey Gitomer, business trainer

## Encouraging the Writing Process

Writing, either narrative or in content areas, should begin as early as Grade 1. The more encouragement students are given to put thoughts on paper, the better writers they will be, and being a good writer is one of the traits of a good student. There are many resources to help teachers with this, and most schools take definitive stances on the writing process, so I will only offer a few hints for strategies I feel are original or different. Helping students to write—to put their thoughts and feelings on paper—is giving them lifelong skills.

> "The mediocre teacher tells. The good teacher explains. The superior teacher demonstrates. The great teacher inspires." — William Arthur Ward

1. Have a set time each week for creative writing. Stick to this schedule as much as you can.
2. Model a piece of your own written work. Modeling is still one of the most effective teaching tools; it inspires students to be like the teacher.

3. Play games.

4. During creative writing time, let students know there is no right or wrong answer when it comes to this type of writing. Encourage emotional involvement by asking questions about how they feel.

5. Make writing meaningful. Let students pick topics, whether it's for narrative or factual writing. You can set boundaries and ground rules, but the final choice must be made by the student.

6. Use exciting prompts to get kids going. There are great websites to help with this; for example, http://writingprompts.tumblr.com/

7. Share creative writing projects, but allow students the option to pass. If a student consistently uses the pass, you need to have a conference to determine the reasons behind their reluctance and together take steps to alleviate the problem.

8. Have students write speech balloons for illustrations and/or create graphic stories; have lots of graphic novels on hand as examples.

9. Teach a few creative writing guidelines; for example:

> The stronger the verb, the better
> Show, don't tell. Let the reader "see" what you mean. Paint a picture with your words.
> Create a mind picture of what you want to say.
> Often reread what you have written to see if it makes sense.
> Think about an author you like and copy some of their ideas.
> Read your writing out loud to yourself. Does it say what you want it to say?

## WRITE-IT-BETTER GAMES

- Fix It: Provide a basic sentence; e.g., *The good dog ran*. Have students in pairs make the sentence as interesting as possible, then share and display finished sentences.

- I Am an Animal: Have students choose the animal they would like to be and think of one describing word to put in front of the name; e.g., Grey Wolf, Lonely Cheetah, Happy Cow. They must come up with other adjectives, related to the one in the name, to describe themselves as that animal. For example, Happy Cow could not use the word *sad*, but could use *laughing* or *relaxed*. Once students have created lists, let them circulate and say only words from their lists to each other; Happy Cow might say *laughing* to one person and *relaxed* to another. This is a fun way to focus on describing words.

- Silly Synonyms: Provide a basic sentence containing several adjectives and adverbs. Have students with partners identify and change all the describers/modifiers. This is a good place to encourage use of a thesaurus. When share time comes, if some of the new words don't quite fit the original meaning, this is the perfect time to discuss how not all words in a thesaurus are suitable for meaning.

- Strong/Stronger/Strongest: Provide a sentence with a basic verb; e.g., *The boy ran*. Have students find better verbs, and list them according to strength value; e.g., instead of *run*, they can use *raced* (strong), *charged* (stronger), *barreled* (strongest). Have them share their words and support their decisions.

**Be aware that praising a poor-quality piece of work can actually do more harm than good, as it conveys your low expectations for the student. Instead, find a small area that is worth praising (even just a title) and then discuss how to improve other parts, and be sure to include your expectations.**

# Venn Diagram Template

Name

Date

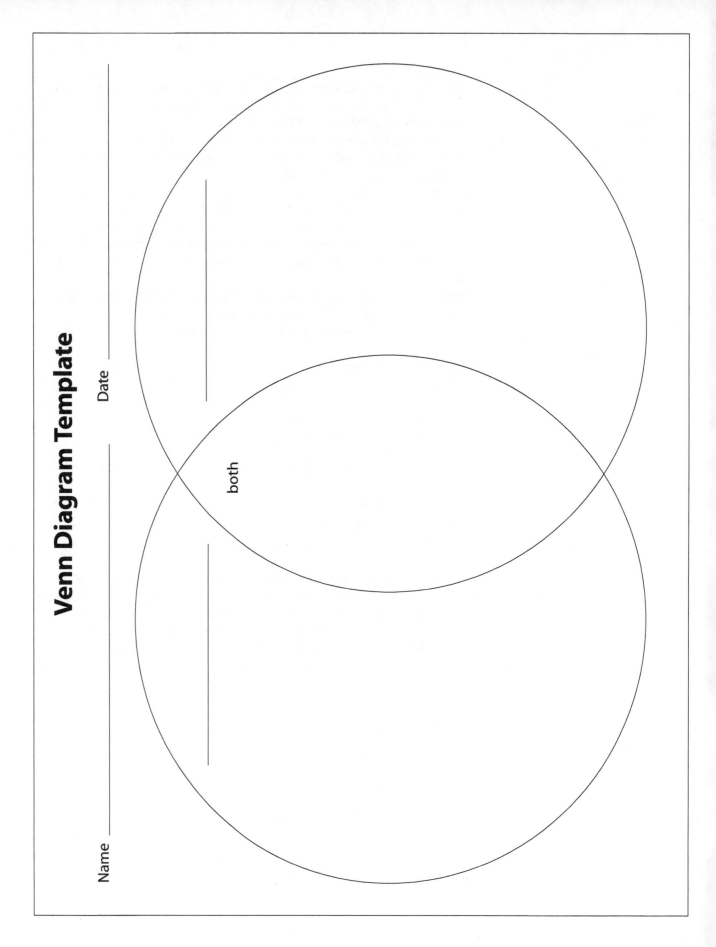

both

Pembroke Publishers © 2019 *The How and Wow of Teaching* by Kathy Paterson ISBN 978-1-55138-342-2

# KWL Chart Template

Name _____     Date _____

| What I **K**now | What I **W**ant to Know | What I **L**earned |
|---|---|---|
| | | |

Pembroke Publishers © 2019 *The How and Wow of Teaching* by Kathy Paterson ISBN 978-1-55138-342-2

# T-Chart Template

Name _____     Date _____

Pembroke Publishers © 2019 *The How and Wow of Teaching* by Kathy Paterson ISBN 978-1-55138-342-2

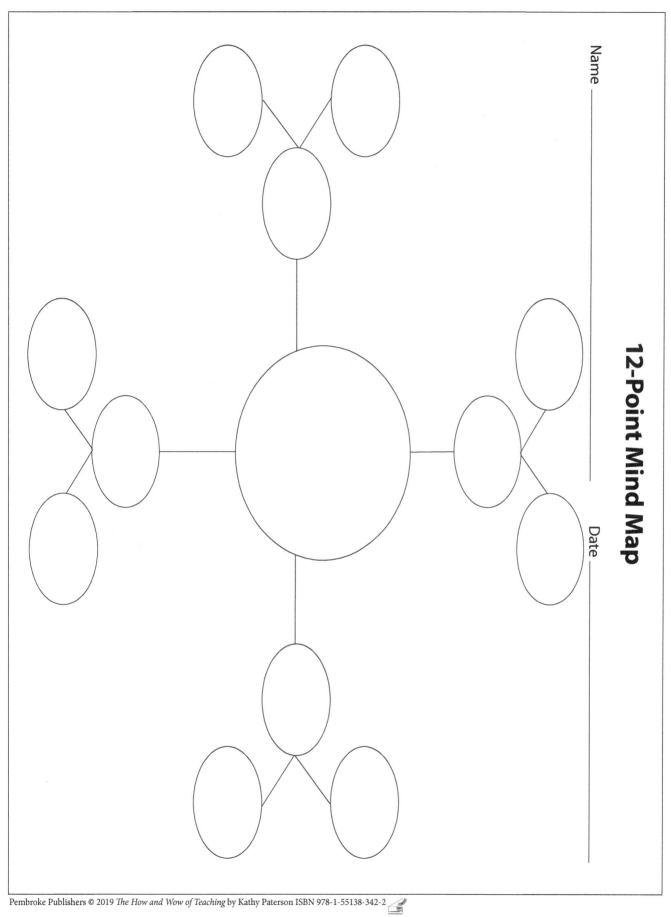

## 12-Point Mind Map

Pembroke Publishers © 2019 *The How and Wow of Teaching* by Kathy Paterson ISBN 978-1-55138-342-2

# Chapter 4 Strategies for Life and Living

"You can't go back and change the beginning, but you can start where you are and change the ending."
— C. S. Lewis

Teaching our students how to live, how to make the most of their lives, how to be fruitful and happy adults is not small task, but it is one with which teachers deal on a daily basis. You may not even realize it, but everything you say, do, think, and share is observed and catalogued by your students. You are, for ten months of the year, their main model for life. A heady thought! But in addition to your mere presence being of such importance, you can, and should, teach specific lessons about life. I know time is always a factor in every classroom—too much curriculum and not enough time to cover it all. But we're talking about the rest of your students' lives here, and taking a few minutes interspersed throughout the week to focus on life skills cannot be anything but good. Teachers can, and should, work toward improving the future lives of their students. Adding wow to teaching means going above and beyond expectations, and when you choose to teach life skills, this is exactly what you are doing. You are delivering a great product and/or service, and students are invited to share the wow of life with you.

## Teaching About Making Choices

We make choices every minute of every day, usually without thinking about them at all. But when the choice is a big one, with big, obvious consequences, it's a different story. We can help students handle these situations more easily. Making the best choices and accepting consequences can be tough for anyone, let alone students, but the teacher who addresses this subject with enthusiasm, excitement, and honest compassion is incorporating the wow factor into the process. When a child suddenly realizes they have a choice, and can make that choice and accept the aftermath, they experience a wow sense of self-satisfaction. There are a few basic rules you can share with your students about making choices.

### Rules for Choosing

#### Simplify the Choice

If there are too many variables, it is harder to choose. Tell students to think of the end picture. What does it look like? Suggest they try not to get distracted by the little stuff and save their decision-making for the big stuff. For example, a student might be trying to decide between two extracurricular pursuits—learning guitar vs playing soccer—because they can only manage one of them. This is a big decision because the end picture will enable them to do only one of two things. The student must simplify the choice by not thinking of the little things like daily practices, playing soccer in the rain, wanting to be with friends, and so on. The student should look to the end result. Do they want to play a game for one season or learn a skill that will be theirs for life?

### Pay Attention to Personal Values

Have students take a minute to figure out their own values. They must ask themselves what is important to their lives. Prompt their thinking by offering suggestions, such as family, friends, education, careers; then suggest smaller values like hobbies and skills, pets, etc. Once students get the idea of considering their personal values, it helps them make better choices. You can also prompt students to think about how their choices affect important people in their lives.

### Learn from the Past

"A failure is not always a mistake, it may simply be the best one can do under the circumstances. The real mistake is to stop trying."
— B. F. Skinner

Tell students to think back and recall if they've ever made a similar choice, and what the consequences of it were. Remind them to try to avoid making the same mistake twice. You might have them make a graphic organizer (T-charts work well; see page 88 for a T-Chart Template) to chart similar past choices and their outcomes. If they cannot think of any past choices, prompt them with questions, such as "What about little choices such as whether to play with___ or ___?" When they can use past happenings to make better choices today, they are developing life skills.

### Look at Both Sides

Have students make a Pro/Con chart for each option. Wherever possible, list all the positives and negatives of the choice. Younger students can do this with illustrations. Often seeing the lists side by side will give the needed incentive to make the choice.

### Ask for Help

Remind students that adults have more experience than they do, and most are willing to offer help and advice. Have them make a list of potential adult helpers to whom they could go for advice with a tough choice. By planning this ahead of time, there is a greater chance they will actually approach one of those adults in the future.

### Don't Procrastinate

"Procrastination is the thief of time." — Charles Dickens
Share this quote with students. They like it, and it seems to have meaning for many of them.

All students know the meaning of procrastination. Your job is to point out how putting off making a choice is never effective. Have them think of a big choice, real or imaginary, then make a list of all the results if they procrastinate. For example, one girl imagined she had to choose between living with her mother or her father. In fact, this was a real and terrifying situation for her. She listed all the possible results of not choosing, one of which was that the courts would decide for her and they'd choose incorrectly. After she put this real and upsetting consequence in writing, she immediately informed her social worker which parent she was choosing. Most students will not face such serious choices, but this anecdote directs attention to the importance of this step in decision-making.

## Accept Your Choice

"One important key to success is self-confidence. An important key to self-confidence is preparation." — Arthur Ashe

This point is all about self-confidence, the confidence of knowing we have made the best possible choice. Tell students, once their decision has been made, to stop worrying about whether it was the right choice or not. Remind them that they have used good decision-making rules, and have given the situation lots of thought, and so now they must stand behind their choice. You might ask students if any of them have ever made a choice, then second-guessed it over and over until they felt ill about the whole affair. Usually a few students will share such experiences; if they don't, share a personal one of your own, real or imagined. It is important for students to acknowledge that a choice made is a choice made. Remind them that they are clever, thinking individuals who went through a rigorous decision process and have made the best possible choice under the circumstances. Learning to trust themselves is a big development step.

## Deal with Consequences

See page 122 for more on consequences.

But what if the end result of a choice is a negative consequence? It is mandatory to talk to students about the acceptance of consequences, not just from choices they have made, but from all aspects of life.

Discuss what the word *consequences* means, then open the conversation by having them consider consequences they might have experienced that that they didn't like. You can prompt with such questions as "Perhaps you stayed up too late and were tired the next day?" "Perhaps you ate too much of something and felt sick?" Have students brainstorm for both positive and negative consequences of choices they have made. Then ask them how they felt when the consequence was negative. They can graphically present their feelings on a chart or with illustrations. The next step is to discuss the importance of accepting those consequences as a part of being a human being and of growing up. The following simple steps may help students to internalize the idea of accepting consequences.

1. Think of why you experienced that consequence. Whose fault was it?
2. Think of how you made the choice. Did you overlook a step in good decision-making?
3. Remind yourself that you are a smart person who made a mistake, and can and will live with the consequences.
4. Take three deep breaths, close your eyes for a moment, and say to yourself, "I can accept this consequence because I am strong and smart."
5. Most importantly, don't whine about it, complain about it, or try to change what has been decided. It will only make you feel bad and make the entire situation worse. Say to yourself, "I know why and how this has happened, and I can deal with it."

# Teaching Organization

Being organized is such a huge aspect of being successful—in school, at home, at hockey practice, or in whatever pursuits students may have—that it truly warrants teacher attention. Any skills for being an organized person you can instill in your students will carry on through the rest of their lives. What a noble undertaking, to be able to help young people with so valuable a skill! Consider seeing an

"For every minute spent organizing, an hour is earned." — Anonymous

extreme state of disorganization, such as the home of a hoarder, completely remedied. This is the incredible feeling students will have when they practice organization, and the feeling you will have when you witness their new sense of order.

## Organization Lessons

The best way to help students learn to be organized is to teach a specific lesson on organization. A great way to begin that lesson is with a personal anecdote about something funny that happened to you due to lack of organization. Teachers all have stories like this, at least partly because we are so busy and have so many people to be responsible for. The lesson should include the following points about being organized.

### Understand Clutter

Clutter is often a cause of stress. It can weigh you down and cause endless anxiety.

Brainstorm everything that might be considered clutter: if you have not used it recently, and are not planning to use it soon, it is probably clutter; clutter is an array of disorganized stuff that you are better off without. The term *entropy* is related to clutter, in that it means the general trend of the universe toward disorder. What this means to us, and to students, is that the process of organizing never stops; it is endless and relentless. Students need to know this important rule of life, as they often think that once something is organized it will stay that way. Next, brainstorm the areas of students' lives over which they have control, that they can declutter: desks, backpacks, binders, bedroom, etc.

Share the following decluttering steps.

1. Remove everything from desk/backpack/toy box/closet/etc.
2. Toss out anything old or not being used. Ask yourself if you really need the item. If not, toss or, in the case of bedrooms and toys and clothes, donate. Make *toss or donate* your mantra.
3. Create a system for what is left. For example, paper sheets go in a file folder, coloring utensils go in a container. Keep to your system of organization. You can organize by size, color, use, value, shape, function—basically any way that works for you. The trick is to stick with your chosen form of organization. You can compare this to *chunking* (see page 34), as they are putting similar chunks of items together.
4. Keep flat surfaces free of anything.
5. Repeat this process weekly to fight entropy.

### Organizational Tips for Students

BE HOME READY

- Pick out tomorrow's clothes tonight.
- Think what you will need for breakfast and lunch if you manage those aspects of your life.
- Keep your work area tidy and organized.
- Declutter regularly. Do the same with your closet and drawers.
- Visualize a tidy bedroom vs a cluttered one.

### ACTIVE ORGANIZATION

- Use routines: Use established school and home routines and create routines for everything else that is important in your life. Make a list of regular activities—e.g., homework, piano practice, play time, etc.—and stick to an established routine. Routines help to offset the stress that accompanies having too much to do and not enough time to do it.
- Stick to one task at a time: Complete one task before starting on another. The idea of multi-tasking has become popular in our too-busy lives, but in fact it leads to disorganization and stress.
- Make lists.
- Make deadlines: When you have a task to complete, especially if it is going to require more than one sitting, make a deadline that is sooner than the actual due date of the task. Deadlines keep us on task and help us to stay organized.

### USE ORGANIZATIONAL TOOLS

- Download a blank calendar one month at a time, and write your routines on the days. Also write down appointments, due assignments, special days, practice times/days, etc. The calendar is a quick check for an entire month at a time. Check the calendar daily and stick to routines. Every weekend do a quick check of the upcoming week.
- Accordion folders are great helpers. You can use them to file materials alphabetically, by subject, or in whatever way works for you. Declutter your accordions weekly. Accordions can be kept both at school and at home and are an excellent organizational tool.
- A planner is like a calendar, but the planner can come with you.

## Organizational Games

These games provide prosocial interaction while organizing students in various ways.

### MINGLE MASH

Students move around the room until you give a stop cue, when they must form groups according to whatever organizational strategy you suggest; e.g., same birthday months, same color shirts, same letter starting first/last name, etc.

### LIFE STAGES

Tell students they are all newborn babies to begin the game. Students mingle, then, on your cue, play rock/paper/scissors with the nearest person. The winners become babies; the losers stay newborns. The students separate into two groups that play against their own members: newborns and babies. The winners in the newborn group become babies and move to that group; the winners in the babies group become children and form a new group. The game continues, with new groups following this sequence of development: newborn, baby, child, teenager, adult, senior. As soon as one or more students become seniors, the game is over. Debrief by discussing how students were organized throughout the game.

In your classroom, you can be a model for good organization. Believe it or not, this starts with personal appearance. Think back to teachers you have had. Some always appeared well put-together, while others appeared disheveled and disorganized. The difference is not in expensive clothes but in an overall calm demeanor of readiness. You can create this look with your style and a smile.

### MORPHING CIRCLES

The goal of the game is to keep forming and reforming organizational groups. Students form a circle with one student, the Caller, in the middle. The Caller calls out characteristics; for example, "red clothes," "likes broccoli," "has black hair," "is male." You can help younger students by providing a list of possible characteristics. All the students to whom the characteristic applies must quickly form another circle. Randomly choose a new Caller for that circle. Through the game, new circles are constantly being formed as a result of different organizational strategies.

### MEMORY ORGANIZATION

Divide students into groups of four or five. Each group has one sheet of paper and one pencil. Display a tray holding 20 to 30 items, all of which can be organized into various groups. For example, the tray could have a pen, pencil, scissors (school); comb, hair pin, hair elastic (hair); soap, facecloth, paper towel (hygiene); and so on. You can use words on cards instead of items, but remember that younger students might need actual items. Tell students they will have 60 seconds to look at all the items and remember as many as they can. Also tell them that the items can be organized in groups and give them the number of groups. Once students they figure out the groups, it will be easier for them to recall more items. Allow students to look, then remove or cover the items. Groups try to recall as many items or words as possible and write them down. The group with the most responses wins.

### SIMPLE GROUPS

"Organization is what you do before you do something so that, when you do it, it's not all mixed up." — Anonymous
I think students can relate to this quote, and certainly they can relate to being organized in their lives. I will never forget the words of a boy who said, "I'm real good at organizing stuff but I need to organize my father so that he stops losing his keys." I wonder if he ever accomplished that.

This game is for younger students. In pairs, students sort a variety of shown objects into whatever groups they think they fit into. Objects can be whatever you have available. The trick is for the students to create appropriate groups and be able to defend their choices. One creative pair put a shoe, a sock, a small shovel, and a sand pail together and called the group Beach Stuff; their explanation was that you take off your shoes and socks to play in the sand at the beach. Pretty hard to dispute that thinking.

### SQUADS

This organizational idea came from Jason Wyatt, who breaks his class into squads for the year. Each squad is very diverse, with a balance of gender, skills, and attitudes. In each squad there is one strong leader, a rule-follower, a logical thinker, an artist, an introvert, an extrovert, etc. The five or six students in a squad develop a shared identity by creating a flag and a chant. When they work in squads, they earn points for strong behavior (dependent on work being done); points are recorded. Competition is kept to a minimum, because the class has shared goals and all are working toward a shared reward; e.g., if the class accumulates 20 rows of points, they get a pizza lunch, dance party, etc. Squad leaders are students the teacher can trust and rely on to help with problems; they sign the agendas of students in their squad, and take attendance (which really saves time on fire drills and in transitions). Students line up in squads and sit in squads at assemblies. Squad leaders can assign points if kids in another squad show star qualities. The squad system is a powerful motivator and great for those students who don't usually get a lot of recognition.

## Time Management

Time management is a hot topic for everyone these days. You may think students do not need coaching about time management, but no one is immune from the pressure of today's hectic world. Even students as young as six years old can benefit from time management training. For the sake of teaching students, time management means the ability to manage daily routines and expectations so as to successfully complete all, or at least most, of them.

### Time-Management Strategies

#### 1. AVOID PROCRASTINATION

Start by telling students to never procrastinate. Point out in any way you can that procrastination is the biggest thief of time: the time not doing what we should be doing is completely wasted, while the issue in question still waits to be addressed. How can students avoid procrastination? Tell them to take a tip from Nike and "Just do it." Try to get students to recall times when they have procrastinated and what the consequences were. Sharing in small groups is helpful. If students can come to their own realizations about how putting things off causes nothing good, they have taken a huge step toward effective time management.

#### 2. PRIORITIZE DUTIES

Start by providing students with an age-appropriate list of duties to be completed in a single day; assume it to be a weekend day. The list could include items like homework, practice, clean bedroom, do chores, etc. Ask students to put tasks into order, most-important first. No doubt there will be differences of opinion; explain that it is acceptable, as we all have different priorities. Discuss why some activities might be more important to complete than others, and lead the talk toward how students can and should prioritize their activities.

#### 3. MAKE A MUST-DO LIST

Students are often good at creating to-do lists, then rushing to check off everything on the lists. Although this is not a bad time-management strategy, there is a better one: a must-do list. This is a prioritized to-do list in which the most important items, the ones that simply must be accomplished, come first. A must-do list is created with the knowledge that if the last things on the list are not accomplished, it's okay. This strategy assures that students will not linger over less-important tasks, and will spend time on the important ones instead. To teach this strategy, provide a list of activities a student might be expected to accomplish on a weekend day. Be sure that some of the activities are unimportant (e.g., watch TV), while others are more important (e.g., practice), and have students decide in pairs which activities could be skipped. Have them star or indicate which activities simply must be accomplished no matter what. Point out to them that we are most focused in the mornings, and if they set out to accomplish the most difficult tasks then, they will be more time-efficient.

#### 4. SET GOALS

Good goal-setting is all about knowing ourselves; anything you can do to facilitate that in your students will help them with more than just time management. Like making a must-do list, this step reminds students to set realistic goals for themselves. This is often a tough one for zealous students who want to do everything all the time. It might require one-on-one coaching with some students in order to help them see what they can and cannot realistically accomplish. In a classroom setting, ask students to answer this question: Can anybody accomplish ____ (specify unrealistic goals), or would it require being superhuman?" Sometimes this wording is enough for them to see that they are expecting too much of themselves. Share these criteria with students:

- Goals must be realistic, something that they really can attain.
- Goals must be measurable, something they can see getting closer and know when the end is near or attained.
- Goals must be important, something that will make your life better or more positive in some way.
- Goals must be time framed, something that can be reached within a reasonable deadline.

A good activity on goal-setting is to have students select two different goals, one that they think is realistic, and one that is impossible to reach. Have them compare the two using the criteria; they can use a graphic organizer, illustrations, or comparison paragraphs. This usually helps them to see the difference between realistic and unrealistic goals.

### 5. CHUNK ACTIVITIES

*Chunking* refers to putting similar activities together for time efficiency. Offer students a variety of tasks, and be sure that some can be chunked: for example, *wash dishes, write thank-you notes for birthday gifts, load dishwasher, do homework, make poster for art, work on science project, practice piano, set the table.* Have students put like items together: for example, they could write thank-you notes at the same desk where they were doing homework and working on science project. These activities can be done one after the other, rather than doing homework at the desk, moving to load the dishwasher, going back to the desk to write thank-you notes, etc. Point out to students that they won't always be able to chunk activities, but it is a worth thinking about when they create their must-do lists.

### 6. AVOID TASK JUMPING

Task jumping might sound like fun, but it refers to the rapid movement from one task directly to another with no buffer time in between. The idea that doing this saves time is erroneous—without a cushion between activities, human beings become less efficient and effective. So share with students the need for time cushions (they like this term) of no more than ten minutes between tasks. What do they do in the ten minutes? Anything they want to. Just knowing they have a time cushion often makes students work even harder during task time.

### 7. DON'T DO HALF—DO ALL

Sometimes, in order to save time, busy students will do a rushed or incomplete job of a task, so as to rush on to the next task. They often say they have to do that in order to complete everything they are required to do. Attempt to persuade them that it is truly better to complete a task well than to half-finish and jump to another task. Explain that if they have prioritized, then it is more important to do

"Once you have mastered time you will understand how true it is that most people overestimate what they can accomplish in a year, and underestimate what they can achieve in a decade." — Anthony Robbins

one job well than two poorly. The issue of problems associated with multitasking can be discussed if desired. Bottom line? One task at a time!

## Money Management

It really is never too soon to talk with students about money management. Even Grade 1 students can understand and appreciate the need for being conservative with money, although some more than others. I realize your influence is limited here, as it's parents who provide (or don't provide) allowances, but you can still talk about smart money management and provide in-school activities that allow the class to earn money for specific goals. Teach your students a few basic ways to better control and govern money when they do have it.

1. Discuss money in class, using age-appropriate examples of use for any money students might have. Also discuss what the class might do with class-earned money; e.g., give to charities, buy resources, use for field trips, etc. Your goal is to help students see that money can and should be used gainfully, as opposed to spending recklessly.
2. Talk about saving. If students have piggy banks, this is a boon. If not, then lead the discussion toward future earnings and consequent saving. Ask:
   - Is it important to save some money? Why?
   - How much should be saved? All? None?
   - What might we save money for?
3. Talk about sharing. Discuss ways students can share money with others. Perhaps come up with a plan to earn and share money with activities such as bake sales, craft sales, doing community yard work, etc.
4. Talk about being a consumer. Conduct a discussion about advertising and how it tries to persuade us to buy things we don't need. Bring examples to class and let students explain to others just how specific advertisements work on our senses and sensibilities. Discuss comparing prices at different stores, even for little items like small books and/or toys. Often a single discussion about consumerism is enough to open young people's minds to its dangers.
5. Talk, especially with older students, about the pitfalls of borrowing money. Open by asking if any of them have ever borrowed money and, if so, how it worked out. Ask: "What happens if you can't pay it back?" and "How would you feel if a friend borrowed money from you and never repaid it?" You can point out that when they are adults borrowing money is different, but even then, it comes with potential perils and troubles.
6. You might choose to open a discussion on how money can't buy happiness. Depending on the ages and interests of your students, this discussion can be very interesting and informative—for both students and you. Keep your goal in mind: to help them see that there is more to life than having money. Of course, if you don 't believe this, skip this discussion. We are all individuals with different needs and interests, and I realize that money is more important for some than for others. On the other hand, you won't get rich being a teacher!

"Money never made a man happy yet, nor will it. The more a man has, the more he wants. Instead of filling a vacuum, it makes one."
— Benjamin Franklin

# Teaching Responsibility

"Responsibility to yourself means refusing to let others do your thinking, talking and naming for you; it means learning to respect and use your own brains and instincts." — Adrienne Rich

How often do we tell students to be more responsible, without considering that they might not quite understand the concept of responsibility? Being responsible means being accountable for something, being dependable, reliable, trustworthy. That's a huge obligation, but we can, and should, help students understand and commit to the tenets of responsibility. Is it possible to teach students to be more responsible? To be more accountable in all aspects of their lives? Certainly we can teach them how to be more responsible at school, and hopefully this knowledge will transfer to the rest of their lives.

1. Start with a discussion about the meaning of responsibility. With younger students, discussion could be prompted by a picture book about responsibility; the Berenstain Bears series by S and J. Berenstain have several that work well. With older students, simply ask for their own definitions of the word and go from there.
2. Have students create a list of actions and activities they think represent responsible behavior. Students compare lists within small groups.
3. Share with students the idea that a responsible student takes an active role in their learning and can be held accountable for their actions.
4. Share a list of in-school responsible behaviors. Make them visible in chart form and have students copy them into journals or notebooks. Younger students can illustrate each step.

## Responsible Actions for Students

See page 126 for a reproducible version of this list.

- Get to school and into class on time.
- Come prepared with your backpack organized, your writing materials available, and your binders in order.
- Pay attention in class. Take notes if required.
- Each evening, go over the contents of your notes and/or backpack as a quick review. This should only take a few minutes.
- Use good time-management skills
- If you are confused about something learned at school, ask for help.
- Study for tests; hand in assignments on time.
- Be honest and trustworthy. This includes keeping secrets. If someone tells you a secret, they are trusting you to keep it. Be responsible; keep the secret.
- Accept responsibility for your words and actions. If you say or do something less than appropriate, admit to it and accept the consequences. Blaming others or tattling are not responsible behaviors. Own your actions.

"You must take personal responsibility. You cannot change the circumstances, the seasons, or the wind, but you can change yourself." — Jim Rohn

This last point is difficult for most students, so more time should be spent discussing it. You might have students write or draw about a time when they didn't accept responsibility for their actions, what happened, and how they felt.

## Showing Respect

Respect is the feeling of admiration for someone due to their qualities, abilities, achievements, etc. We frequently tell children to respect their elders without asking if they really understand the term. This was brought to light when a young boy was asked if he respected his teacher and replied, "I think so. What does that mean?" Teachers should indeed talk to and with their students about the issue of respect.

1. Begin with a definition of respect solicited from the students. Make a list of words they feel relate to respect. Once again, with younger students, there are many lovely picture books about respect that work as good lesson openers.
2. Share your definition of respect. Use specific examples, some that show respectful behavior, and some that do not. Provide the examples and have students decide why or why not they show respect. In this way, you make the abstract term more concrete for them. An example of respect could be *The boy opened the door for his grandmother*; an example of lack of respect could be, *A girl accepted a candy from her mom and walked away.*
3. Discuss who we should respect and why. Students may not appreciate the fact that they should respect their peers, the younger children and themselves, as well as their elders. This can be a heady discussion, but once students are aware of the true nature and purpose of respect, they are more apt to be respectful to everyone.
4. Share a list of respectful behaviors.

## Respectful Behaviors

**See page 127 for a reproducible version of this list.**

- Be polite. Use your manners all the time with everyone.
- Listen to others when they talk. Make eye contact; pay attention.
- Pay compliments when and where they are due.
- Be sympathetic to others. Think about their rights and feelings.
- Treat others fairly. Take turns.
- Respect yourself. Know you are a valuable human being worthy of respect, but remember that if you want respect, you've got to give it first.
- Accept others just the way they are. Remember that everyone is different, and everyone is beautiful in their own right.
- Maintain a positive attitude and be open-minded to new ideas that others may have.

**This single point can become an entire unit of study.**

- Respect the environment by not littering, polluting, tramping on protected wilderness, etc.
- Respect your school by not writing graffiti, littering, destroying or misusing property or tools, sticking gum anywhere, etc.

**"Respect for ourselves guides our morals; respect for others guides our manners." — Laurence Sterne**

- Avoid teasing or using profanity, bad language, and sarcasm.
- Remember the Golden Rule: Treat others as you want to be treated yourself.

## Respect Activities

### THE TREE OF RESPECT

Have students draw a bare-branch tree that encompasses an entire page (older students) or provide a page with such a tree photocopied on it (younger students). The tree should have as many branches as possible, with small branches branching from larger ones. On or at the end of each branch, students draw leaves. In each leaf they print the name of someone they respect. The more leaves the better, so that students have to think beyond family, teachers, people they see everyday. This visual helps students to see that everyone they know deserves respect.

### NARRATED TOY STORY

This is a role-play improvisation with boundaries. The boundaries are that each toy is initially disrespectful of the other toy until the appearance of the Respect Fairy. To make this more age appropriate for older students, toys can be replaced with superheroes, famous athletes, or pop stars.

1. Divide the class into groups and explain the scenario:

   *In your group, each person is a toy as from the movie* Toy Story, *and one person is the Respect Fairy. I will be the narrator who tells the story while you act it out. You will be acting out lack of respect, then respect. Be sure to make the two actions very different.*

   Older students may be able to be their own narrators.

2. Allow groups a few minutes to choose roles and talk about how to show respect.

3. Bring each group to the front and narrate a story:

   *The toys were all playing and talking*
   (pause for action)
   *when one got a ball and refused to share.*
   (pause for action; encourage disrespectful behavior)
   *One toy tried to stop the arguing and make a suggestion, but the others were rude and didn't listen.*
   (pause for action; encourage dialogue)
   *One toy began to cry and the others all made fun of it.*
   (pause for action; encourage dialogue)
   *Suddenly, along came the Respect Fairy. She talked to them about their behaviors.*
   (stop for action and dialogue)
   *The toys felt terrible. They all tried to change their ways and act more respectfully.*
   (pause for dialogue and action)
   *The Respect Fairy asked them how they were feeling then.*
   (pause for dialogue)

4. Debrief after all groups have acted by discussing their feelings when they were disrespectful, and then when they were respectful.

### TWO-FACED CLOWN

Have students divide a page vertically and draw a clown face on each side, one side depicting a clown showing disrespect, the other showing respect. For example, the disrespectful clown could be sticking out his tongue, sneering, scowling. The respectful clown could be smiling, giving a thumbs up or a peace sign. Have students name each clown and share their depictions with the class, explaining how each clown is showing respect and disrespect.

### RESPECT OR DISRESPECT?

Share a number of scenarios with students and have them decide if there is respect or disrespect involved. If the scenes are disrespectful, have students change them to make them show respect. Here are a few samples, but you will want to customize your stories to the age and experience of your students.

Your teacher asks you to clean up and Bobby runs to his desk.

An elderly gentleman comes to listen to students read and Keisha tells him he is old.

Ravi's aunt comes to visit and Ravi sits and listens to her talk, even though he is bored.

Jonny needs to blow his nose but has no tissue, so he quietly picks his nose and wipes his hand under his desk.

Saria tells her friend a secret and her friend tells her mom.

### RESPECT BUBBLES

Tell students they have imaginary bubbles around them, and no one can enter those bubbles without permission. Have them walk carefully around, avoiding each other's bubbles, occasionally stopping and asking permission to enter another's bubble to shake hands/hug/etc. Remind students that they can say no, but should do that respectfully also. Debrief by reminding students that they have the right to say no to others, even to adults, for things such as tickling/hugs/ kisses/etc. if they don't want bubble invasion. Also remind them: Respectfully saying no is the way to go.

### FRAGILE FEELINGS

**Check for egg allergies before using this activity.**

This is a fun activity for outside! You will need a raw egg for each child, and a few extra. Each student prints an emotion on their egg. Students share what they have written and add whether it is a negative or positive emotion. Then you tell them that all emotions, negative and positive, have something in common—they are very fragile. Have students carefully carry their eggs outside to a place where raw egg will not be a problem, or where it will be easy to wash up with a hose. (I usually get the cooperation of the caretaker beforehand and he is ready with hose in hand. In the winter, this is less of a problem because eventually the eggy snow disappears.) Have children stand in a circle and put their eggs on the ground in front of them. Randomly call names, and the students you call throw their eggs to each other and try to catch them. Eventually all the eggs will be broken. It's messy fun and a very visual reminder that emotions are fragile. Debrief by discussing what we can do if we break someone's emotional egg; i.e., cause emotional distress for another person.

### I SPY RESPECT

Give students a homework assignment to find and report back a given number of examples of respect they see in the neighborhood, in the playground, at home, etc. Being alert to respect makes students more respectful themselves. It's all about awareness.

## The Wow of Teaching Self-Regulation

By dealing with issues of self-regulation in your classroom, you are incorporating into your teaching a crucial element that enhances the lives and experiences of your students. You are creating wow for them by giving them life skills; you, yourself, will experience the wow when you see them moving forward with control and self-awareness.

## Handling Emotions

As a teacher, you are with your students daily, most days of the week, and you see them experience a wide variety of negative emotions and even emotional meltdowns. One of the most important things you can teach your students is about those pesky emotions and how to cope with them.

1. Discuss emotions. It is a good idea to point put that emotions are "of the heart"; they are what make us human beings and special, diverse individuals. Share with students that it is good to talk about feelings, to share them, to look at them critically and try to figure out how to make them work for us, as opposed to against us.
2. Use a T-chart (see page 88 for a T-Chart Template) or similar organizer to separate positive emotions from negative emotions when students feel them. Brainstorm as many different emotions as possible, then divide them into positive and negative. Pay attention to the fact that even the negative emotions have something positive about them; for example, fear can protect us from danger, and sorrow can prepare the way for happiness later.
3. Point out that everyone experiences both positive and negative emotions, and all people handle them differently. You might ask students to share examples of how others (no names, please) did or did not handle an emotional outburst. It is important for students of all ages to be reminded that strong negative emotions are a normal part of life—that everyone experiences them and that we can learn to manage them.
4. Ask students to pick the negative emotion that worries them the most, and either draw a picture of it (maybe as a monster) or write a paragraph about it. This promotes self-awareness, a step in the development of emotional intelligence. If students learn to identify emotions that are problematic for them, to name them, they can also learn ways of coping.
5. Select a few of the most common negative emotions and discuss with the class possible ways to deal with them. Discuss coping strategies. This might take several minilessons, but the time spent is well worth it. It is not necessary to specifically examine every negative emotion students suggest. Point out that the basic coping strategies work for all situations where emotions take control.

## Coping Strategies

Before discussing coping strategies, provide students with a printout or a picture depicting each strategy so that they have both visual and auditory input for the discussion. Point out that students can pick and choose from various coping strategies. Share all the strategies, discussing each. Keep reminding students that everyone will have a few coping strategies that work for them. Share your personal coping strategies if you feel comfortable doing this; it can help make the situation more real to them. When you have gone over the entire list, give students some time to consider which strategies might work for them. Have them rewrite these choices, illustrate them, journal them—whatever is appropriate for your class.

- Recognize the emotion you are feeling. Is it anger, rage, fear, sorrow, frustration, worry? Give it a name and say to yourself, "I am feeling___!" Naming the feeling gives you some control over it.

- If necessary, remove yourself from the room or area to a quiet and secluded spot nearby. If this is not possible, simply sit on the floor, hug your knees, close your eyes, and move on to your chosen coping strategy.
- Close your eyes and take three deep breaths, letting each one out as slowly as possible. Try to see and feel the air as it leaves your body.
- Imagine yourself inside a beautiful bubble filled with peace and love. The bubble gently lifts you up and moves you in a soothing, peaceful manner.
- Hold a "go-to" object or article. This can be a stuffie, a pillow, a small trinket, a blanket, a sweater—whatever makes you feel better. If you often feel strong emotion at school, keep your go-to object in your desk or backpack.
- Keep your eyes closed. Imagine you are in a warm, safe place. If you find a place like this in your mind (real or imagined), always come back to that same place when you need to calm your mind.
- Hum a favorite tune in your mind. Hum it over and over and over, saying the words silently if you can.
- Touch your thumb to each of the other fingers on that hand in sequence while saying the words "I–feel–at–peace," one word per finger. Repeat several times.
- Do a personal reboot. Close your eyes. Imagine you have a connector port on the back of your neck and when you plug into that, your entire body reboots. Practice this strategy by closing your eyes, feeling the plug being connected, feeling the jolt your body gets on the reboot, and feeling the following sense of calm.
- Laugh! If you have a joke book handy, read it. Laughter is good for chasing negative emotions, but it is not always easy to break into laughter at school. So the at-school alternative is to make your belly smile. This is a rather silly trick but it works. Close your eyes and focus on your belly. Try to make your belly into a big smile by contracting and releasing belly muscles.

## More Coping Strategies to Teach Students

### POSITIVE SELF-TALK

Creation of self-talk mantras makes a great minilesson. Once students have created their mantras, have them poster them, illustrate them, do whatever is necessary to get those mantras well into their memories so that they can be readily accessed in emergencies. Possible self-talk mantras:

I am strong and beautiful.
I can do this because I am strong.
I am calm and relaxed.
I am powerful and in control.
I am peaceful inside.
I am not alone and not afraid.
I know who I am and I am good.
I am important.
I am allowed to say no.

### BRAIN CUSHIONS

Sometimes our brains feel overloaded to the point where we simply lose control and negative emotions take over. Ask students if this has ever happened and discuss what it felt like. Suggest that they imagine a beautiful soft cushion morphing all around their brain. Tell them to close their eyes, feel the cushion, give the cushion a color, and just rest within the comforting support of the brain cushion. Maintain silence for up to two minutes, occasionally prompting them to feel the cushion. Debrief by discussing what it felt like, and where/when they could use that strategy.

### ACTIVE REPETITION

This strategy can be a bit noisy, but for some students it is remarkably soothing and allows them to regain emotional control. Have them copy a short physical sequence of actions, such as *stomp, stomp, clap* (stomp one foot, then the other, then clap once) and repeat the action over and over until calm has returned. The action needs to be both simple and repetitive. Have students create their own sequences, share, and practice together. Tell them to pick their favorite and stick with it. It needs to be an activity that can be used naturally and without concentration.

### REPETITIVE SOUNDS

Like repetitive actions, sounds repeated over and over in the mind tend to be relaxing and calming. Use the scale for teaching this strategy, having them repeat *do, re, mi, fa, so, la, ti, do* in their heads. All students know these notes and can mentally repeat them easily. Do a few repetitions aloud together as a class, then have students close their eyes and repeat the notes in their minds. If students have different sounds they like better (one girl hummed the alphabet song tune) that is fine too.

## Dealing with Negative Feelings

Most emotions can be managed using the previous coping strategies, but a few strong sentiments might require separate strategies. These are the overwhelming feelings of hurt and embarrassment, both of which students experience at school from time to time. When feelings are hurt, you are given the opportunity to discuss with students the next step, forgiveness.

> Both hurt and embarrassment involve humiliation, perhaps the most difficult feeling for students to handle. Humiliation can be defined as the lowered feeling of self-worth and reduced status experienced when others are around. We don't feel humiliated when we are alone. It is a feeling dependent on the presence of others.

### EMBARRASSMENT

Embarrassment is a feeling of discomfort, of agitation, even of disgrace. It occurs as a result of something done either by the person experiencing the feeling or by someone close to that person. It is widely associated with the familiar face flushing but, in fact, many people do not blush at all. You can help students learn to deal more effectively with embarrassment.

1. Start, as with teaching about any emotion, by discussing the feeling. Share an incident where you were embarrassed. Ask students to share as well, but be ready for a lack of response, because even talking about being embarrassed is embarrassing. So share a few examples of embarrassment, real or imaginary, to get them thinking of the feeling.
2. Ask what it feels like inside when one is embarrassed. Try to draw out words like *nervous, worried, lonely, picked on, worthless*, etc. You might ask students of all ages to illustrate what embarrassment looks like using abstract drawings and color.

3. Ask what kinds of things cause us to feel embarrassed. Again, be ready with your own examples. Point out that the behaviors of others can cause embarrassment to us, too. The Robert Munsch book, *I'm So Embarrassed* is a good lead-in to this discussion.

4. Talk about the fact that feeling embarrassed is a normal emotion that everyone experiences. Give students a few seconds of silence to think about a time they were embarrassed.

5. Ask students what they did when they were embarrassed. Be prepared to share how you handled that situation yourself.

6. Share coping-with-embarrassment strategies. Talk about each one separately, and point out that students should find the best strategy or strategies for themselves.

- Own It: The first thing to do is take a big breath and figure out exactly what you said or did to cause the embarrassing situation. It might be as simple as being associated with someone who did the embarrassing act. By naming and owning the act, you will have taken a huge first step.

- Move On: As soon as you have owned the moment, the next step is to move on. You may want to offer an apology, but otherwise just "shrug and scoot." In other words, acknowledge the moment then move on to something else. Avoid constantly apologizing or bringing up the situation. It happened in the past. Be in the present.

- Use Positive Self-talk: When the situation is well over, do not beat yourself up with talk like, "Oh, I'm so stupid. I should have…" Instead, say to yourself, "It wasn't that bad. It's in the past." Practice saying this a few times.

- You Are Who You Are: Remind yourself that you are not perfect. We get embarrassed when we think the reactions of others indicate what kind of person we are. We judge our self-worth by the behaviors of others. When you think about it, this is silly. Being perfect is impossible, and if we stop trying to be perfect, we will be more accepting of our flaws and our humanity. Because we are human, we make mistakes.

- Stop Ruminating: Some people just keep going over an embarrassing situation in their minds, long after it has happened. Have you done this? There are two facts to remember about this:
    1. Others are not judging you; you are judging yourself.
    2. The past is past. You are in the present. The embarrassing situation belongs to the past.

- Laugh at Yourself: Many embarrassing moments are actually quite funny in retrospect. Think of an embarrassing moment and to try to see the humor in it. Look from the outside in and see what the situation looks like when you are not involved.

### HURT FEELINGS

Young children tend to throw around the accusation, "You hurt my feelings" without really understanding what they are saying. But they do, in fact, often suffer from hurt feelings. You can help them learn to understand and cope with these negative feelings.

1. Talk about feeling (emotionally) hurt. What does this mean? How do we hurt each other? What does it feel like to be hurt? What does it feel like to hurt

**Isn't *ruminating* a lovely word? Students like to hear it, so use it with them to make a point about dwelling on past mistakes.**

someone else? Point out that hurting someone else willfully is an inappropriate behavior. Acknowledge that sometime we hurt others without meaning to.

2. Share with students that often the hurter is feeling emotional pain themself and that is the reason for the inappropriate behavior. Tell a student who has been hurt to try to see why the other person(s) did what they did.

3. Tell students to use words to tell how they are feeling. Practice short phrases, such as "You hurt my feelings by…" "I am hurt because…" Help students verbalize exactly how and why they are feeling hurt. Often just by saying it out loud, the situation is defused.

4. Tell students to ask themselves what they might have done to create the situation. At first most students will adamantly say, "Nothing!" Closer introspection can lead them to see that they did, indeed, have a part in the incident that has caused them hurt feelings. Learning to identify personal involvement is a huge step in coping with hurt feelings.

5. Remind students that in all situations they have a choice. When they are experiencing hurt feelings, they can choose to be a victim and stay hurt, or they can choose to move on and feel the joy of life. This may seem a bit speculative and insubstantial to young people, but if you discuss as a class how they can move on, they usually take it to heart and will remember these strategies:

- Stop feeling sorry for yourself now! Make a conscious decision to let it go.
- Tell yourself you are okay.
- Make yourself smile, even if you don't feel like it.
- Say out loud, "I forgive you for hurting my feelings."
- Physically move away, even just a short distance, from the spot where it happened.
- Immediately get involved in something else, even just journaling.

### HOW TO HELP STUDENTS LEARN TO FORGIVE

Most teachers will have heard a child say adamantly, "I don't forgive you!" Children use this statement as a form of power or control, and they don't actually understand the huge concept of forgiveness. We can and should teach to that.

1. Open the lesson by saying, "If I accidentally lost all your pictures/projects/papers/etc. would you forgive me?" Go with the flow of the discussion and lead it to a reasonable definition of the word *forgiveness*.

2. Invite students to share a time when they did or didn't forgive someone. Let the discussion go where it will, but then direct it to the idea that in order to forgive, one has to be strong. This important point often shocks students, who don't associate forgiving with strength. Explain to them that, in order to forgive, you must be strong enough to move on. Ask students if they believe they are strong enough to move on from a situation where forgiveness was necessary.

3. Discuss the idea that forgiving doesn't mean forgetting. Nor does it mean you are giving the other person permission to do it again. What it does mean is that you are strong enough to leave this particular happening in the past and move forward with your own life. For, in truth, unless you forgive the situation and realize it's over, you cannot move forward yourself.

4. Tell students to stop blaming; start being more self-aware. Blaming others is easy and very foolish. It shows weakness of character and lack of self-awareness. By sharing this information with students you are giving them

"Our prime purpose in this life is to help others. And if you can't help them, at least don't hurt them."
— Dalai Lama

"Forgiveness is not an occasional act, it is a constant attitude."
— Martin Luther King, Jr.

another tool for managing forgiveness. Tell them to try to look into themselves and see that they are actually allowing the other person to control their emotions. By forgiving the assumed wrongdoers, students are taking control back. The saying "People can only hurt you if you let them," rings true here, although it may be too abstract for younger children to understand. Simply tell them that by forgiving, they are taking control.

5. Let the anger go. Discuss how we can release our anger in healthy ways, rather than by holding blame and resentment in our hearts.
   - Visualize a STOP sign when you feel the anger inside, and when you see that sign, make a conscious effort to think of something else.
   - Breathe deeply and slowly, and repeat to yourself, "I am in control. I am not angry."
   - Close your eyes; tense, then relax your entire body. When tensing, try to hold every single part of your body, even your hair, tightly. Then relax completely and be like a bowl of jello. Repeat several times.
   - Be very active. Run! Jump! Skip! Do something active, even in the classroom, for a full minute. This is an instant anger release.

> "For every minute you remain angry, you give up sixty seconds of peace of mind." — Ralph Waldo Emerson

## Emotional Awareness Activities

Helping students learn better emotional coping techniques, increasing their emotional intelligence, is a worthy goal for all teachers. I wish you good luck in your endeavor to make the citizens of tomorrow better, more grounded, more emotionally stable individuals. This section offers a number of activities, or games, that can be used in all grades and at any point in the curriculum. They are designed to draw students' attention to their feelings, and therefore be better able to understand them, and communicate about them. In addition, they are fun. Enjoy!

### BOOK OF WARM AND COLD

This is a whole-class activity that is ongoing and appropriate for all ages. Provide each student with a scribbler. On the front print *Hot* and on the back print *Cold*. Discuss how some things that happen every day make us feel good, peaceful, or happy; that is, warm. Other happenings might make us angry, or unhappy; that is, cold. Give examples from your life. Then show students how to record each happening in either the Warm or the Cold side of the book. The Cold side starts at the back and moves toward the front. The Warm side starts at the front and moves toward the back. When they meet in the middle, it's time for a new book. Encourage students to decorate both sides of the book according to the implications of Warm and Cold. Then have them record one item in each section. This can be a sentence, a short paragraph, an illustration, or just a few words. My single rule for this book is that every time a student writes a Cold, they must also write a Warm. In this way, students are forced to see that there are good things happening even when it feels all bad. You can skip this rule, of course, and allow random creating. Just let students know this is not a diary, and therefore you will be reading their books from time to time. What you do with the books is entirely up to you, but you will quickly see that students become more aware of their daily feelings.

### INSIDE OUT

Watch the wonderful Disney movie *Inside Out* with students of any age and follow with age-appropriate activities that allow students to delve into emotions and emotional reactions. This can be as simple as pointing out the various emotions from the film, or as complex as doing research reports on emotional intelligence.

### EMOTIONAL METER

Have students draw a thermometer with five points on it. Label the lines, beginning with 1 at the bottom or bulb of the thermometer:

5 Exploding
4 High
3 Controlled
2 Low
1 Calm

Discuss how emotions can fall in to any of the points on the thermometer, but the higher they go, the more difficult they are to manage. Have students tape the thermometer to their desks or work spaces and, at random points throughout the day, have students identify a current emotion and rank it. They can keep a record of different emotions and their temperatures for about a week, at the end of which have a discussion of emotions: some emotions occur more often, some are more explosive than others, all are natural, etc. It is always interesting to rank an emotion when something exciting or disturbing happens in class. This helps students get a visual understanding of emotions.

### INTERACTION DETECTIVES

Have students spend a break (lunch, recess, etc.) silently watching others and identifying their possible feelings. Like detectives, students should carry notebooks and jot down points. No names are to be used, even if they know the names of the people they are watching. Debrief this activity in a sharing session in which students share one of their findings and try to justify their beliefs regarding the feelings being projected.

### ME, MYSELF, AND I

Discuss words that can be used to describe ourselves, not physically, but emotionally. Instruct students: "Ask yourself if you are generally a happy person. A frustrated person? A quiet person?" Brainstorm (especially with younger children) words that describe people according to their personalities and emotions. Once you have a lengthy list, have students write the following lead sentences on a page, leaving lots of space between each sentence.

1. These are three words that I think describe me:
2. These are three words that describe what others think I am:
3. Words that are different in #1 and # 2 are
4. Why I think they are same/different:

After completing the lead sentences, students either write or illustrate the *Me I Want to Be*, based on the personal observations plus the observations speculated of others. The final projects should be shared and displayed.

## THE CLOUD

Have students imagine they are clouds. Talk them through this, using cue words such as *soft, foggy, absorbent*. Tell them that every time someone says something negative to them, they will simply let it melt into the cloud and feel no effect whatsoever. Have students draw or write about their clouds, what they look like, smell like, feel like, etc. And remind them that they can go into their clouds whenever they need to.

## EYE-SPY

This activity gives students practice in making eye contact and in recognizing the emotions that go with that.

1. Have students mill slowly, avoiding all eye contact with each other.
2. Have them stop after one minute and sit where they are. Ask them to share how that felt.
3. Let students mill again, this time making brief eye contact then immediately looking away.
4. Have them stop, sit, and discuss feelings. Compare this with what they have done to real life, when they want someone to look at them and they turn away.
5. Have students mill and make eye contact with each other. As soon as they have made contact with another, students are to stand beside that person and avoid making eye contact with anyone else.
6. Students stop, sit, and discuss. Compare what they have done with real life, when two friends avoid everyone else. How does it feel when they have a friend? When they didn't have a friend?
7. Debrief with discussion about the importance of eye contact. Have students create posters illustrating the many ways and places eye contact is important.

## HASHTAGS

A hashtag is a label for content, a word or phrase preceded by a the hashtag (#) symbol. They provide a means of the public expression of sentiment. Once per week (or at your convenience) write a hashtag on the board and invite students to respond in their journals or on index cards that can the be pinned to the board with the hashtag. Use hashtags that focus students' thinking on their emotions:

#WorstDayEver
#BestMomentEver
#MostEmbarrassingMoment
#MostDorkyMoment

Invite students to come up with their own hashtags and watch this activity take off. It allows students to focus on their feelings and share them with others.

## IT'S A FEELING!

Have students bring to school three or four pictures from newspapers, from magazines, downloaded from Internet, etc. The only stipulation is that there must be a person and/or animal in each picture. Once you have a good collection of pictures, pick a couple at random and discuss. Ask what the character might be feeling and why. Encourage different responses, then debrief by pointing out that we all have different ideas about how others are feeling and so shouldn't jump to conclusions without more information. Have each student choose one picture, glue it to a lined sheet of paper, and write a single sentence indicating how the character is feeling and why they think that. For example, *The cat is feeling frightened because his tail is up.* Pass the pictures and pages around and have other students add their own comments; if they can't think of anything different to write, they pass the picture on. Eventually you will have a set of pictures complete with different explanations that can be displayed and discussed in class. This can be an eye-opening experience, showing that students can expertly support different claims.

## Your Diverse Classroom

"We are all different, which is great because we are all unique. Without diversity life would be very boring." — Catherine Pulsifer

As every teacher knows only too well, each student in a classroom is a unique individual with traits and characteristics that separate them from all the others. The diversity within a single class can be of race, gender, sexual orientation, physical/intellectual abilities, spiritual beliefs, socio-economic standing, ethnicity, political beliefs, degree of parental support, and more. Yet every student must be treated fairly, as impartially and as benevolently as possible. Take a moment to consider the magnitude and multifariousness of this. Dealing with diversity is a huge element in your job description as a professional educator. George R.R. Martin said, "Different roads often lead to the same castle." This is a simple way of thinking of the teaching experience. You set students on miscellaneous routes and hope they all reach or surpass your goals for them. As teachers we need to understand and accept the wide diversity within our classrooms and instruct with that always in mind. Being a "diverse" teacher in a diverse classroom simply takes a little creativity and forethought. It begins with making the students aware and accepting of diversity, and then constantly tapping into that awareness in all subjects and activities.

1. Have an open discussion about diversity. This discussion can and should be repeated every year with every class, as awareness grows and biases tend to develop. Point out that strength lies in differences, not similarities. Celebrate diversity. Make a class poster to which each student adds something personal. Students can make pictures of their heritage, their likes, their dreams, etc., cut them out and add to the class diversity poster. Display the poster proudly.

2. Get to know your students individually through two-way *Me* journals. These are scribblers used only for back-and-forth talk between student and teacher. Students are given a few minutes at the end of each day to write about themselves. This is different from other journaling because the prime purpose here is for students to share something personal through words or illustrations. Entries could include

   - anything about home/family/pets
   - anything that happened that day at school
   - feelings, desires, upsets from the day
   - suggestions, ideas for future school days
   - grievances, annoyances, general thoughts
   - fears, anxieties
   - happy thoughts, good happenings

Once a week, read the Me journals and take time to respond to each. This may seem time-consuming; in fact, it can be done in about 30 minutes, and it is time very well-spent. You will learn so much about your students that instructing them will ultimately be easier.

3. In addition to Me journals, having students fill out an interest inventory early in the year can be very enlightening (see page 128 for a School Survey). Not only will it give you motivational ideas for the rest of the term, but it will also allow you to better appreciate the diversity and similarity among your students. I suggest a simple yes/no survey that even non-readers can complete with parents or helpers. It can include questions that are specifically content-related, such as "Do you like reading?" or more general, such as "Do you belong to an after school team or club? If yes, what?" Keep these questionnaires and refer to them throughout the year.

4. Use a variety of teaching strategies (see Chapter 3). Obviously, you cannot provide individual instruction all the time. The more methods, approaches, tricks, and techniques you use in your classroom—that is, the more diverse your teaching itself is—the more students you will reach.

5. Do random checks for involvement. Make sure every student has equal opportunity to learn, take part, discuss, offer examples, contribute, show their work, etc. Some students tend to disappear into the background and often these well-behaved ones are overlooked simply because they are good. Make *equal opportunity* your mantra.

6. Include a wide variety of learning materials and resources in your classroom. Remember that, while one student might learn from listening, another might require a visual representation, while a third might need to use physical manipulation.

7. Include reading materials that touch on the many diversities of the world, such as language, race, culture, gender, age, etc. These materials should be available to all students in a reading corner, and should be a large part of what you share when you do your daily reading to the class.

8. Celebrate cultural holidays. We are blessed with such a multicultural mingling of students in our classrooms that celebrating as many cultural occasions as possible just seems natural. This doesn't have to be a big deal. Merely bring information about the special day into your regular literacy lesson for the day. One elementary school has a regular Heritage Day, for which students come dressed in costumes representing their varied heritages. Another has instituted a Grandmother's Life Day for which every student in the school writes and/or illustrates a story depicting a day in the life of their grandmothers. This provides a multicultural masterpiece for school display.

9. Learn about parenting styles from different cultures. This is strictly a teacher task. If you better understand the differences in parenting styles, your relationship with the student and their parents will improve.

10. Study the world! This seems like a foolish point to have to make, but it is a reminder to include information about our amazing planet and all its natural diversity of humanity whenever we can. Need a story book to read? Choose one of the many multicultural ones, such as Sesame Street's, *We're Different: We're the Same*, or *All the Way to America* by Dan Yaccarino, or (my personal favorite as it deals with both cultural and socio-economic diversity) *A Chair for My Mother* by Vera B. Williams. Students of all ages can and do appreciate a picture book. (I have used them successfully with university students who watched and listened raptly.) As long as you are enthusiastic and read with

passion, they will attend. One school does a wonderful postcard activity: students' friends and family are invited to send postcards from everywhere to the students at the school. Then the class locates the source of the postcards and the teacher uses these teachable moments to provide a little cultural information.

## Managing Student Behavior

Every teacher knows the frustration and annoyance that comes when a student interrupts the normal flow of a lesson with a difficult, often inappropriate action. Probably that same student disrupts on a regular basis. Constantly dealing with these students is a major cause of teacher stress, and can actually erode teacher confidence and cause classroom upheaval. It is important to realize that most students don't feel good about "being bad." There is something at play behind the behavior; if you can figure it out, it can become an important step in dealing with it. We can't just assume they are being bad on purpose. Still, you still have to somehow handle the inappropriate behaviors. When managing difficult students, whether they are one-time or repeat offenders, there are a few simple rules to follow.

**How-to-Wow Managing Difficult Behavior**
- **Establish a relationship.**
- **Promote responsibility.**
- **Maintain a safe classroom.**
- **Use proximity.**
- **Be consistent.**
- **Set clear expectations.**
- **Never give up.**

1. Start with a relationship. It doesn't take long to figure out where the classroom problems lie. As soon as you identify the student, do whatever you can to form a positive relationship with them. This is your first line of attack. Teacher Jason Wyatt was able to build trust and relationship with three difficult students: the first he asked to teach him how to play the guitar, and the once negative-attention-seeker became an incredible instructor; another troublemaker was asked to help pick out a scooter for the teacher's son, and the student was calm and sociable; a third student was really getting into trouble when the teacher asked him about choosing the right antivirus software for his computer, and the student complied beautifully. The truth is that difficult students often just need to build a relationship over something that matters to them.

2. Spend some one-on-one time and just talk. Principal Stacy Fysh uses a wonderful technique she calls the *What else?* strategy

   Tell me about you.
   What about _____ makes you uncomfortable?
   What else is upsetting you/do you need help with/is bothering you/etc.

   Continue asking "what else?" until the student runs out of ideas. Stacy uses this in place of a problem-solving approach and has found it to be very successful with all manner of inappropriate behaviors.

3. Figure out the student's interests.

4. Figure out the student's red flags: situations, times, things, activities, persons that set them off.

5. Make a point of speaking directly to the student every morning, after breaks, at the end of the day. Just a few simple words using their name will suffice. No matter how busy you are, take the 30 seconds to do this.

6. Make eye contact with the student frequently throughout the day. Make sure it is positive eye contact, not eye contact affiliated with a look of concern or displeasure.

7. Ask for their help. Be sincere. Solicit the student's help for something they can do that you cannot.

8. Promote responsibility. Of course, this is important with all students, but especially with the difficult ones. Ask for their input, have them make choices, and give them small in-class duties, such as keeping the back table organized.

9. Maintain a safe classroom (both emotionally and physically) where no one is picked on or singled out in a negative manner. Discuss this with the whole class and have them think of examples of actions that lead to a classroom feeling unsafe, then think of alternate behaviors. Sometimes a difficult student is also one disliked by others, and is consequently left out. Discuss individual responsibility for making everyone in class welcome. On the other hand, especially among older students, sometimes the difficult student is revered, looked up to. Again, class discussion is warranted, but this time about being individuals, not following bad examples, being strong and true to what we believe in. Keep bringing the topic back to the safe classroom.

10. Build on little successes. Once again, this is a good rule for all students, but especially for the difficult ones who often suffer from too much failure and too little success. Be on the alert for the tiniest improvements in physical, emotional, intellectual behaviors and quietly comment on them to the student in question. Do not make a big deal of this or other students might react negatively. A quiet whisper, a nod, a gentle touch on the arm will suffice. Later, during your one-on-one with the student in question, you can elaborate and specifically tell the student what they did that you liked.

11. Use proximity. As much as possible, keep the student near to you. This is a natural strategy for a teacher; you do it instinctively. But continue it everywhere out of the classroom as well: on field trips, in the playground, in the gym, at assemblies.

12. Use consistent disciplined practices. Explain to the whole class that if X happens, then the consequences are always Y. During your one-on-one with the difficult student, reinforce class rules and consequences, and add others that specifically apply to that student. Always keep the consequences exactly the same, and always verbalize them when using them. For example, "You were late after recess. You know that the consequence of this is that you must go to the office for a late slip." With the difficult student, identify their particular problem behaviors and establish consistent consequences for them.

13. Have very clear expectations. Again, the whole class benefits from this, but especially the difficult student who may need constant reminding of those expectations. Tie your expectations to your teaching goals and try to make them realistic, so students understand the *why* of the learning. For example you might say, "This math is difficult. You will have to think carefully. But once you have it figured out, you'll be able to divide money, or toys, or goodies, whatever you want, quickly and equally."

14. Never give up. It is tempting to just give up on difficult students, to let them be and to focus our energy on the ones who are actually going someplace. I encourage you not to do this. Take a little time out if you need to. Ignore the student for a day or even two, but then get right back and be their mentor, boundary keeper for negative behavior, rewarder and supporter of good behavior. In this way, you are creating little positive wow situations between you and this student.

*"It's not what we do once in a while that shapes our lives. It's what we do consistently."* —Anthony Robbins

- Worry Stones: Principal Stacy Fysh keeps worry stones on her desk. If a student is sent to the office for discipline, she tells the student to take three big slow breaths, then to pick up a worry stone and put it in their pocket. She then explains that when the student is upset, they should rub the stone in their pocket. All this takes place prior to discussion of the reason for the student's office visit. One time a very disruptive boy later returned with three peers, all asking for worry stones, and the boy in question was much more settled from then on.
- Dot Connect: The student is given a sheet of paper and two different-colored felt pens. They are asked to quickly put as many dots on the paper as possible using one color. Then they have to connect as many dots as possible with the other color. The random, unthinking action often reduces stress and calms the student.
- Sharp Angles: Similar to Dot Connect, the student is given a sheet of paper and a felt pen. For this activity they are asked to draw overlapping triangles all over the page as quickly as they can. The rapid drawing of the sharp angles forms tends to be relaxing.

## DEFIANT STUDENTS

A defiant student is one who openly resists, who simply refuses to follow directions or rules. Sometimes, other students see their defiant peers as being strong and worthy of following. Consequently, it is important to deal quickly with defiant behaviors and defuse them.

First and foremost, realize that there is an underlying reason for defiance. There is a condition called Oppositional Defiance Disorder, in which genetics and brain function play a part. Faced with this, it is necessary to work with parents and sometimes with medical professionals. But for students who do not have the condition, the most common reason for defiance is the feeling of power the student gets from the reaction of teacher and peers. This is good news! Remove the reaction of others and defiance dies out.

1. Remain calm and neutral. Practice patience and see if the outcry dies on its own.
2. Talk with the class (with the defiant student present) about how people who display defiant behaviors are seeking power, and how we all have the power to not react. Shift the power to the other students. Sometimes just talking about this in class helps to defuse the defiant student. Talk about *acting* as opposed to *reacting*: as a class watches an act of defiance, choose to return to your work and ignore the defiant student, as opposed to laughing or watching or in any way reacting to the student.
3. If/when a student shows defiance, call it what it is and give the student an easy out—offer a quiet place. For example, "You are being defiant. Please step outside the room for a minute until you can rethink your behavior."
4. Avoid power struggles; you will lose. Use a calm, defusing behavior, eye contact, a quiet voice, and a consistent offering of a way out. Remember that the removal of your attention is the biggest deterrent to defiant behavior.
5. During one-on-one talks, set realistic consequences for acts of defiance, and remember that consistency is the key. What are realistic consequences? These should be age-dependent, but a few examples are

- immediate removal to the hall/corner/carrel/principal's office to calm down
- student to take a breath, move to the back table, and write in their journal
- immediate exclusion from the discussion to a quiet place previously selected
- imposition of a penalty, such as missing recess, having to write an apology, helping with some school duty that they would not otherwise be involved in

6. Avoid the student's attempts to bargain or give excuses. Keep your position of power by calling it like it is and setting the established consequence(s).
7. Look for positives. As with any difficult behavior, make a concentrated effort to find and acknowledge positives with the student. These can be behavior-related, work-related, etc.—just be sure to acknowledge them specifically ("Good job of focusing on that math question until you got it" as opposed to "Good job.") and with sincere appreciation in your voice. Also consider the occasional positive note home.

### STUDENTS WHO ACT OUT

Acting-out behavior is difficult to define, as it encompasses a variety of patterns and actions. It may present as fighting, throwing fits, screaming, having meltdowns, or stealing, to name a few. It is an out-of-control activity that somehow gives emotional release to the student. Sometimes it is a one-time behavior, while at other times, students may act out so regularly that people literally tiptoe around them. One little girl in Kindergarten had a meltdown, complete with screaming, hiding, and hitting, almost three times a week. Her concerned teacher and principal were at their wit's end. This type of inappropriate behavior is usually caused by suppressed or hidden feelings or emotions, and usually the child themself isn't even aware of them. Thus, managing them in a classroom becomes a difficult chore.

1. All the suggestions for dealing with difficult behavior apply here but, in addition, stay extremely calm and quiet, and avoid giving a lot of attention to the child during the acting-out phase. Remember, your attention is what fuels the behavior. When this happens in a classroom, you must take instant action for the sake of the rest of the students, so that action should be immediate removal (in any way possible) of the acting-out student to a predetermined quiet place.
2. Teach the child coping strategies. These will differ according to age, but you can work with child and parents to establish a series of steps or strategies the student can be reminded to use during an acting out episode. These might include

- having a blank sheet of paper and black marker and scribbling
- punching a pillow
- deep breathing with eyes closed
- shaking a tambourine or hitting a small drum
- popping bubbles on bubble wrap
- pinching each fingernail in rotation with the forefinger and thumb of the other hand.
- pinching both earlobes while quietly repeating "mamamama"

"When we long for life without difficulties, remind us that oaks grow strong in contrary winds, and diamonds are made under pressure." — Peter Marshall
If a student is feeling despair due to inappropriate behaviors, share this quote.

3. When the acting-out episode is over, take time to talk to the student about their feelings. Ask what they were feeling, what words describe it, what part(s) of their body felt it, what color(s) the feelings were, etc. Finish by reminding them of the coping strategies they have used and how they work. Give positive reinforcement for the use of the coping strategies.

4. Ask for help if necessary. It's okay to admit defeat and turn to professional medical personnel when you feel you are not being successful handling the situation. Be sure the parents are in on this with you. Never go behind their back, even if it's with the best interests of the student in mind.

5. Reassure yourself that it is not your fault. Sometimes, as teachers, we feel we can handle everything and, if we can't, then we are somehow responsible for that failure. This is not the case. Give it your best compassionate and consistent effort. Don't give up on students or on yourself, but be willing to step back and get help.

### ANGER

Anger is a basic human feeling that is often associated with shame and/or guilt. While the feeling of anger is completely normal, the ways with which it is expressed are not necessarily always appropriate. There are steps that can be taken to help students better cope with this strong, often upsetting emotion.

1. Stay calm. Of all teacher interventions, this is the most important. No matter what you are feeling, stay calm, speak calmly, move slowly, maintain eye contact, make sure your body is showing calmness. Be very aware of your nonverbal communication. Breathe slowly, thinking *calm* on every exhale.

2. Stay emotionally detached. Whatever the student is saying and/or doing is not aimed at you personally. Remember, you are the adult in the situation.

3. While a student is in the throes of anger, avoid trying to enforce consequences or touch them. Either may actually inflate the anger. Instead, observe placidly, stay close, and wait until the outburst has calmed a bit before proceeding.

4. Reassure and calm the student. Don't try to discuss what has happened or what will happen right now. Instead, if necessary, use statements such as

> I can see how upset you are.
> You are obviously frustrated and angry.
> Take a big breath and we'll talk about this later.
> You are upset. We'll talk later.

5. Remove the student only if necessary. If you can easily steer the angry student outside the classroom or away from peers, do so. If this is going to cause more discomfort, just deal with the situation where it is.

6. When you talk with the student later, be supportive, as opposed to punitive. Let them know you understand how upset they were, and what a nasty feeling that is to experience. Listen carefully, with full eye contact and open body language. Discuss coping strategies and better ways to deal, even if it was a one-time occurrence.

7. Let the student know you will need to contact their parents. Document the situation and contact the parents only after you and the student have agreed on a coping strategy should it happen again.

"Anger is an acid that can do more harm to the vessel in which it is stored than to anything on which it is poured." — Mark Twain

Sometimes students exhibit anger in ways that are aggressive and hurtful and/or harmful to others; this is considered aggression. If this happens at school, if the anger has escalated to potentially harmful aggression, the teacher is required to step in. First and foremost is the safety of the angry student, as well as that of everyone else. Keeping that in mind, there are steps you can take.

1. Be loud and assertive. Using a piercing voice, demand the student stop whatever they are doing immediately.
2. Tell other students to move away and sit down. Use a no-nonsense voice.
3. Send a student for help only if you cannot control the situation yourself, and then do this is a calm, matter-of-fact manner.
4. Using a calm, unthreatening, and noncombative manner, speak to the aggressive student and tell them firmly to stop immediately. Use physical restraint only as a last resource. If you must use physical restraint, the most effective position is to stand behind the student and quickly grab both their hands while crossing them in front of them so that you are holding them firmly, with your arms like a straitjacket. If necessary, slide to the floor, still holding the student in this manner.
5. Allow the student to vent and say what they are upset about. Watch your nonverbal communication (no crossed arms or facial scowls), assuming you are not physically restraining the student. Remain calm.
6. Time out the student if necessary, in the room (if there is a quiet corner), the hall, or the office. Tell them they can return in 10 minutes or whenever they feel calm.
7. Follow the incident with a one-on-one talk. Instead of acting angry (this is what the student will expect), be supportive. Accept the reasons for the outburst without question, but lead the talk to better ways of coping.
8. Avoid forcing an apology. Forced apologies are superficial at best, and anger-provoking at worst. Instead, suggest that apologizing would be a good idea, but leave it up to the student. If they do apologize on their own, provide specific positive reinforcement.
9. Remember to record the incident in writing, and have all students involved do the same.

LAZY BEHAVIOR

The term *laziness* refers to the inability or refusal to do work or expend energy. The word suggests procrastination, unfinished tasks, late assignments, etc., and definitely has a negative connotation. But if really look into the lives of those we consider lazy, we might find completely different reasons and considerations for their behavior. Perhaps we need to consider extenuating factors, such as what we are asking of them being misunderstood or too difficult, the student experiencing anxiety related to possible failure or not being good enough, or some other equally significant barrier. Keep in mind that no one wants to be lazy; it causes feelings of incapability and ineffectiveness, and annoys, even angers, others. Being lazy isn't a choice. It is a condition that actually makes life more difficult for the person in question. This suggests we should look at laziness as a reaction, not an action, so we can take steps to alter that reaction.

1. Provide clear directions. Ask the "lazy" student to repeat them back to you. Go to the desk of that student to be sure they completely understand what is

"The secret of getting ahead is getting started." — Mark Twain

to be done and what the first step is. The first step in anything is always the hardest. Getting the student to take that first step will help them to be more industrious.

2. Set and constantly reinforce classroom expectations. Let all students know when work is expected, exactly what they should be doing, and exactly what the consequences are for not doing it. For example, "For the next 30 minutes you will be working on the rough drafts of your reports. I expect everyone to be writing and researching—nothing more. If you are not following these instructions, you will be invited to join me after school to make up double the time wasted in class."

3. Be extremely consistent. Say what you will do and do what you say! No surprises.

4. Form a relationship with the "lazy" student. In one-on-one time, explain what you are concerned about (late assignments, time wasted in class, etc.). Avoid using the word *lazy*. Invite the student to brainstorm with you to figure out ways to remedy the situation. Do this together as a team. Then reinforce their attempts to utilize the strategies.

5. Consider peer tutoring. I don't mean tutoring for the "lazy" student, but for them to tutor someone else. This sense of responsibility is often all a student needs to be more actively involved in school. The student being tutored can be younger, which will instill role-model attributes in the older student.

6. Give the student as many realistic responsibilities as possible. If the "lazy" student has low self-esteem, you can boost their feeling of self with higher expectations of them. For instance, have them do some sort of paper work for you (not recording marks—privacy first, please) or delivering to the office or other classrooms.

7. Always (and this goes for all students) make sure students are aware of exactly how/when/where school learning will affect them directly in their lives. Avoid the "Why do we have to learn this stuff?" questions by providing the reasons first. I overheard a teacher saying, "I wasn't sure myself why they had to learn that, so we just set it aside until either I could figure it out, or we forgot it entirely." Correct way to handle the tricky question? I don't know, but I do know the teacher handled it and gained a little respect from her students.

### LACK OF INTEREST

Uninterested students are a huge problem that causes undue teacher stress. Lack of interest generally refers to being uninterested in pursuing a task, possibly due to lack of understanding of how it will immediately affect the individual. Lack of motivation has an even more negative connotation, and refers to a pessimistic view of chances of success. I have lumped the two together here, as the tips for handling each are similar. Students in these categories tend to be negative, to forget about the benefits of success, and to be excellent excuse-makers and blamers. It is your job to turn their lack of interest around—to motivate them.

1. Be sure your good teaching practices (clear expectations and consequences, good directions, enthusiastic delivery of lessons) are in place.
2. Get to know the student to see if there might be an underlying reason for the apparent lack of interest.
3. Invite all students to offer opinions frequently, to take part in what they are learning and doing, and to make choices. In this way you are helping the uninterested student feel more a part of the group, and giving merit to their ideas.

4. Students love to interact with peers. Use this knowledge to have them work in groups, to have a say in their own learning, to feel responsible for what happens in the classroom. Make learning meaningful.

5. Find out what interests the uninterested student and incorporate it into classroom work if possible. One teacher discovered that a totally uninterested 10-year-old boy loved a particular online game. She set up a literacy task for which students had to research and write about the merits of this game and compare it to an offline game. It was a huge success and the uninterested boy was in the front of the pack.

6. Use *baby steps* with the uninterested student. If a half-hour of homework totally turns them off, ask for 10 minutes, then gradually increase the time. Point out exactly how the homework is helping them.

7. Stay in contact with parents and be sure to communicate any small positive steps taken. Do whatever you can to boost the student's confidence both in and out of school.

### WITHDRAWN SHYNESS

This student is quiet and shy, and seldom interacts with others. The unfortunate reality of our larger classrooms today is that these are the students who too often receive the least of the teacher's time. They do not interrupt the class. They do not ask for help. They can easily be ignored when so many others are squeezing every breath from the teacher. How can we help these students? First, it is important to look at why they may present in this manner. The shyness can be a part of the overall personality, or it can be situation-specific; e.g., reaction to loss, feelings of failure, disappointment, etc. Whatever the cause, you can use intervention strategies that will help the student be more outgoing in class, and hopefully in life in general.

1. Use peers. Pair up students and be sure to pair the shy student with an appropriate, sensitive student who will be compassionate and not pushy. Use the buddy system frequently.

2. Use proximity when teaching or during class discussions to keep the student focused and to encourage a feeling of safety.

3. Use small groups for activities, always checking to see if/how the student interacts with the group.

4. Engage the student in special activities. For example, have them take or pick up messages to/from the office. Give them a special role, such as daily math book monitor. The nature of the role is unimportant; it is the fact of the consistent expectation that helps boost self-confidence.

5. Avoid placing the student in a situation that might cause stress or embarrassment. An example might be oral reading to the class. If you want the child to take part in this, provide the selection ahead of time and practice it with them, inviting at-home practice. Then ask the student quietly if they are ready before calling their name.

6. Use peer preference in seating. If there is a particular student with whom the shy student does interact, sit them close.

**See page 129 for an interest inventory specifically for withdrawn/shy students.**

7. Use interest inventories (see pages 128 and 129) to determine the student's interests and find ways to capitalize on this information.

8. Teach the student about parallel play. This is playing whatever the group is playing, only alongside or near to them instead of with them. Avoid telling the shy student to ask if they can play; the possibility of peers saying no is

strong and it will make the shy student feel worse. Instead, use words that indicate the shy student is doing the same thing as the rest of the group.

9. Help the student learn how to deal with social rejection. Explain that all kids get rejected sometimes, that it doesn't mean that others don't like them. Explain also that even teasing doesn't mean they are disliked, and that the best way to deal with teasing is to say, "That really hurts," then walk away.

10. When the student doesn't respond to a peer's question, help them by using phrases like, "They are thinking and will probably answer that later." Avoid using the term *shy*.

11. Have opportunities in class to discuss things you know are important to the shy student. If the student does share, use specific positive reinforcement and later, in one-on-one talks, remind them of how well they did in that discussion.

## PHYSICAL LIMITATIONS

At some point in your career, you will have a student with physical disabilities in your class. It may be a short-term disability, such as a broken arm or leg, or chronic disability, such as cerebral palsy or cystic fibrosis. More seriously disabled children usually have full-time aides accompanying them, but you must plan to include them in classroom activities. Some of the ways to do this are obvious, and I include them here simply as reminders in case you are expecting a physically disabled student in your class. Just remember that you can be a real boon to that student's welfare and educational development.

1. First consider the physical environment. Make the area as safe as possible by removing obstacles and having clear passage to/from the student's designated working area.

2. Discuss disability with the class (it's okay if the disabled student is present), using the stance that we can choose to remove the *dis* from *disability*, and be left with *ability*. Point out that we are all unique, all important and valuable. *Disabled* does not mean *less able*. It means unique. Have all students make a list, chart, or illustration showing their personal uniqueness. This works with students of all ages. I did this with university students and later received a thank you note from a student in a wheelchair, who said no one had assumed that position before and it made him feel special.

3. Speak directly to the student at their eye level, and not to the assistant if there is one.

4. If it is a temporary disability, invite the student to share feelings, fears, etc. with the class. Other students are always curious about disabilities. By giving the student a platform, you are satiating curiosity and boosting the self-confidence of the disabled student. Some chronically disabled students may want to do this too, but you will need to check with them beforehand, so as not to embarrass them.

5. If possible, choose electronic versions of courses and readings. If this is not possible, provide print material and course outlines in advance so that the disabled student is never in a state of not knowing what is going on.

6. Don't forget that these students require positive reinforcement for achievements. Keep your feedback sincere and specific. A preadolescent girl in a wheelchair was seen tearing up an award paper and tossing it away. When asked why she did this, she said, "I got it for good work in math. I hate math. I don't even try and I suck at it. So this is a phony award." Be careful. You

can't fool kids. Give reinforcement, but make it real. Better for the girl in the wheelchair to have received the award for admitting she hated math. At least then she might have laughed, and maybe even tried harder in math.

7. Be aware of the extent of the physical disability. Can the student raise a hand? If not, then be alert to eye contact and remember to call on that student intermittently.

8. Discuss respect with the whole class and together create a poster of ways to show respect to each other. Sometimes kids want to do the right thing, but are not sure how to go about it.

9. Talk with the student about what they can and cannot do. Don't assume. You may need to offer alternative ways to handle assignments, but never assume the student doesn't want to do it; for example, don't assume a student doesn't want to present orally, even if they suffer from speech problems. Be flexible and accept suggestions from the student themself.

10. Use your best teaching strategies. Include manipulatives and visuals in content lessons. Employ several senses at a time when coaching a new skill. Be enthusiastic and use a loud, clear voice, especially when giving directions. Be the great teacher you know you are!

## Teaching Consequences of Misbehavior

**See page 92 for more on consequences.**

A consequence is a conclusion derived through logic, its importance lying in its ability to produce change. Think back to consequences you might have received as a child. Were they logical? Fair? Did they encourage you to make behavior changes? Chances are, you answered no to at least one of those questions. Think of a student standing in a corner with a dunce cap on their head. A natural consequence? I think not. More likely the action of a teacher who had tried every other trick in their handbook and was frustrated and fatigued. What would the child learn from that, other than humiliation? Thank goodness we know much more about the value and nature and outcome of consequences today. We now know that consequences must be logical, natural, reasonable, and related to the problem, so that both student and adult can maintain self-respect.

A natural consequence is one a child has imposed on themselves. For example, if they refuse to eat breakfast, and then is hungry midmorning, that is a natural consequence. If they fail to complete homework, and the teacher makes them stay after school to do the work, that is a logical consequence. Do natural and logical consequences work? They do if the following criteria are met.

### EFFECTIVE CONSEQUENCES CHECKLIST

A consequence is most effective if

- it is directly tied to the inappropriate behavior.
- the student knows exactly what to expect and what the behavior was that brought about the consequence.
- it is carried out in calm, assertive manner. Remember you are the role model for behavior.
- it allows student to save face; it doesn't lower self-esteem.
- it is focused on future improvement, not past misdoings.
- it allows the student to learn something and move forward.
- the entire situation remains positive; consequences are used to help the student make better choices and not as a punishment.

## NEGATIVE CONSEQUENCES

Although the term *negative consequences* has a bad connotation, there are times when a negative consequence is probably the best intervention. While positive consequences are used to reward good behavior, negative consequences are used to discourage bad behavior. Both should be used in a classroom, but the latter is in a grey area, surrounded by doubt and indecision. Teachers sometimes have difficulty establishing effective consequences for inappropriate behavior, and may even have limited, or no, parental support. Yet the teacher must take action when a student misbehaves consistently. The teacher must work with the student in question and establish a set of rules and natural consequences if they are broken.

A negative consequence should

- be something the student considers unpleasant, such as loss of a privilege.
- be applied immediately after the misbehavior.
- be applied in such a way that the student is reminded of the misbehavior, the broken rule, and the appropriate behavior expected as a result of the consequence. For example: "You failed to do your homework again. You will remain after school in the principal's office for two consecutive nights to complete the unfinished work and also do an additional page. I know this will help you to finish homework on time in the future."
- be applied keeping the student's dignity intact (no frowns, negative body language, put downs, etc. from the teacher).
- help the student learn to be responsible for own actions.
- be followed with positive reinforcement. For example, following their first after-school work: "I am pleased to see you went straight to the principal's office and got to work. That shows me you have good work habits so I know you'll be able to apply them to your homework from now on."

**"Do the best you can until you know better. Then when you know better, do better." — Maya Angelou**

### SUGGESTIONS FOR NEGATIVE CONSEQUENCES

- Group reminder: letting whole class be aware of rules
- Individual reminder
- Lunch or recess detention
- Time out: in class, with appropriate work assigned, such as writing assignment explaining what happened
- Time out: in office, with assignment
- Parental referral
- Temporary school expulsion
- Permanent school expulsion

**These are provided in order of severity. The assumption is that the most gentle consequences (simple oral reminding) will always be tried first.**

Keep in mind that whatever consequence is used, the goal is to teach the student better ways to behave and to return to the classroom with their self-esteem intact. When using negative consequences, always pair them with appropriate positive consequences as well.

### POSITIVE CONSEQUENCES

Teachers everywhere know these as positive reinforcement, and are well-versed in their merits. However, it's important to keep in mind that the most meaningful element of any intervention, positive or negative, is the importance of the reward to the student. Finding rewards, or positive consequences, that are fair, effective, and as natural as possible can be a challenge. Technically, a positive consequence will increase the frequency of positive behavior. The most common positive consequences used in classrooms are

- tangible: stickers, food rewards, money (allowance at home)
- social: specific teacher praise, letters of accommodation sent home, awards and rewards, full-school acknowledgment
- activity-related: more free time, game time, gym time, time to talk with peers

POSITIVE CONSEQUENCE ACTIVITIES

No matter what the diversity in classrooms, no matter the degree of emotional and physical heterogeneity, there are a few failsafe ideas that help keep classrooms under control. These might be considered positive consequences for negative behaviors, but in fact they are designed to remove otherwise resistant negative behaviors.

- Intercom Call: Have disruptive students, after a predetermined time of good behavior, find silly knock-knock jokes, share them with you (to be sure they are appropriate), then read them over the intercom at the beginning of the day. This responsibility seems to be enough to deter at least some negative behaviors.
- Door-to-Door: Have the problem student(s), after a predetermined period of good behavior, find a short joke or funny anecdote that is then shared with you. Then at a pre-selected time, the student goes door to door (doors of cooperating teachers only; some may wish to pass), knocking, entering, sharing the joke, then leaving for the next class. The positive reinforcement gained from peers and teachers can help curb further inappropriate behaviors.
- Tech Time Bank: Students of all ages love technology, especially when that means playing games. After a predetermined period of good behavior, students earn points that are banked. Once a predetermined number of points have been banked, the student "buys" a certain number of minutes of free tech time, during which they are allowed to play teacher-monitored games.
- Home Rewards: Work with the parents and establish a reward for the student after they complete a designated period of appropriate behavior. The inappropriate behaviors should be listed so that parents, student, and teacher are fully aware of the expectations of the cessation of these behaviors. The home rewards could be increased allowance, screen time, later curfew, reduced chores, etc.
- Whole-Class Rewards: This is where the whole class earns a reward based on the behavior of one student. If the problem student can keep it together for a predetermined amount of time, the class can earn 20 minutes computer time/10 minutes extra recess/10 minutes free play in the gym/etc. The student in question is given social support because you point out that they have earned a reward for everyone.

## Proactive Measures

As a final word on dealing with disruptive students: often proactive measures are the best. The following are a few such measures taken by principal Stacy Fysh at her school.

1. Hair gel and mirrors are available in all classrooms, as it was discovered boys were frequently leaving the classroom to check their hair.

Stacy Fysh suggests using a One-Minute Intervention with students who have been struggling. Simply make eye contact, say one or two specific positive words (e.g., "Great hair today") and keep going. This quick seek-and-greet intervention is often enough to get the student through the day.

2. Flexible seating for work is used. This means students can choose to work anywhere within teacher awareness and sight. They can sit on the floor, in the corners, under cupboards, on tables—as long as they are working.

3. Kid Connect: Every kid connects best with one teacher in the school. Teachers need to be aware of which students connect with them, and be there to support these kids even if they are not in their class. This total attachment can be used to offer support and reinforcement all year long.

4. Togetherness Puzzle: Although this action actually follows a disruptive incident of students fighting, it is proactive in that it prevents future occurrences most of the time. When two students have been fighting, the principal immediately brings them to a quiet place and has them work on a simple puzzle together. Sometimes it is a chore they have to do together, or even a project. Rather than questioning or punishing them for the fight, the principal explains that the students have to live together so they need to get along, and working on something together helps that. They can return to class when the activity is successfully completed.

# Responsible Actions for Students

- Get to school and into class on time.

- Come prepared with your backpack organized, your writing materials available, and your binders in order.

- Pay attention in class. Take notes if required.

- Each evening, go over the contents of your notes and/or backpack as a quick review. This should only take a few minutes.

- Use good time-management skills

- If you are confused about something learned at school, ask for help.

- Study for tests; hand in assignments on time.

- Be honest and trustworthy. This includes keeping secrets. If someone tells you a secret, they are trusting you to keep it. Be responsible; keep the secret.

- Accept responsibility for your words and actions. If you say or do something less than appropriate, admit to it and accept the consequences. Blaming others or tattling are not responsible behaviors. Own your actions.

# Respectful Behaviors

- Be polite. Use your manners all the time with everyone.

- Listen to others when they talk. Make eye contact; pay attention.

- Pay compliments when and where they are due.

- Be sympathetic to others. Think about their rights and feelings.

- Treat others fairly. Take turns.

- Respect yourself. Know you are a valuable human being worthy of respect, but remember that if you want respect, you've got to give it first.

- Accept others just the way they are. Remember that everyone is different, and everyone is beautiful in their own right.

- Maintain a positive attitude and be open-minded to new ideas that others may have.

- Respect the environment by not littering, polluting, tramping on protected wilderness, etc.

- Respect your school by not writing graffiti, littering, destroying or misusing property or tools, sticking gum anywhere, etc.

- Avoid teasing or using profanity, bad language, or sarcasm.

- Remember the Golden Rule: Treat others as you want to be treated yourself.

Pembroke Publishers © 2019 *The How and Wow of Teaching* by Kathy Paterson ISBN 978-1-55138-342-2

# School Survey

Please answer all the questions as well as you can. Use the back if you need more space.

1. Do you like reading or being read to?  ❑ Yes  ❑ No

2. Do you have any brothers/sisters? If so, what are their names?

3. What is your favorite TV show?

4. Do you have a favorite online game? If so, what is it?

5. Do you belong to an after-school sport/club/team/activity? Please tell me about it.

6. Do you have a pet? Please tell me about it if you do.

7. What is your favorite school subject?

8. What is your least-favorite school subject?

9. Do you have any chores at home? If so, what are they?

10. Who is your favorite pop star?
    Movie star?
    Superhero?

11. Who is your real-life hero?
    Why?

12. What kind of music do you like?

13. What do you like to do after school?

14. Tell me about one goal you have for the future.

Pembroke Publishers © 2019 *The How and Wow of Teaching* by Kathy Paterson ISBN 978-1-55138-342-2

# Interest Inventory for a Withdrawn/Shy Student

*To be filled out by parents/guardians for younger children.*

1. Do you have a best friend in class? If yes, who?

2. What is your favorite place to sit in the classroom?

3. What is your favorite toy/item at home?

4. What kind of music do you like?

5. What is your favorite school subject? Why?

6. What is your least-favorite school subject? Why?

7. Do you like recess? Why or why not?

8. Who is your favorite person?

   Why?

9. Tell me two things that upset you in class.

10. Who would you most like to sit beside in class?

11. What kinds of stories do you like to read?

12. Who is your real-life hero?

13. When are you the most happy?

14. What do you want to be when you grow up?

Pembroke Publishers © 2019 *The How and Wow of Teaching* by Kathy Paterson ISBN 978-1-55138-342-2

# Chapter 5 Teacher Responsibilities

"One looks back with appreciation to the brilliant teachers, but with gratitude to those who touched our human feelings. The curriculum is so much necessary raw material, but warmth is the vital element for the growing plant, and for the soul of the child." — Carl Jung

Being a teacher involves so much more than just teaching. Teaching is a "many hats" role with a myriad of responsibilities. This chapter will look at a few of those responsibilities with the intention of sharing tips and techniques for how to manage and simplify that important role. Max Forman wrote, "Teachers are those who start things they never see finished, and for which they never get thanks until it is too late." Just consider how many different things you start every day. You inspire with questions, you awaken joy in creative expression, you arouse natural curiosity, you assist with discovery. You reach unattainable goals with inadequate tools. You are amazing. Allow me to support your amazingness with tips for handling other professional duties.

## Marking

Realistically speaking, no one likes marking, but it is a professional responsibility and obligation that cannot be overlooked or reduced in importance. This applies all the way from Grade 1 to post-secondary institutions. Marking must be done with a purpose and with the student's individual progress always in mind. Is it possible to reduce marking time and still implement quality student feedback? I think it is. The way to begin efficient and effective marking is, I believe, to obtain a full repertoire of marking tips and techniques. Sometimes just being aware of a few different ways to assess can make the task easier. Novelty is good.

Can marking wow students? It can, and often does. When care is taken to make the marking a little bit personal, students will be thrilled. Consider a simple comment on a Grade 4 writing assignment: "Billy, you made this sound so great I want to go there. Can you pack me in your suitcase next time?"

High-quality marking and constructive feedback are your professional responsibility, and your greatest gift to your students. Take a tip from Dr. Seuss: "Unless someone like you cares a whole awful lot, nothing is going to get better, it's not!" Marking, assessment, and feedback are under the quality-of-teaching umbrella. You, too, can become a master marker with a bit of effort and a love of teaching.

Of course, not every piece of work requires in-depth, full-focus marking; in some cases marking specifics will be enough. Nevertheless, marking can, and often does, become a stressful, arduous task. Let me share some ideas to help mitigate and simplify this extremely important teacher task.

### Why Mark?

- student and teacher feedback
- evaluation of student growth and future needs; to monitor progress
- self-evaluation for teachers on lesson effectiveness

- criteria for reporting to parents, students, educational institutions
- reinforcement and motivation for students

## Marking Basics

**How-to-Wow Marking**
- **Use the same place, a positive attitude, and a timer.**
- **Chunk the marking and choose a strategy.**
- **Skim first.**
- **Focus (avoid interruptions).**
- **Set realistic goals for yourself.**
- **Record both marks and your time goal.**

Marking will never go away, but you can make it more time-efficient and yet still effective. Attack marking the same way you teach students to attack homework. Marking and homework are so similar that teachers often refer to their take-home marking as homework. Here are a few tips to keep it as simple as possible.

- *Mark in the same location as much as possible.* Whether it's the kitchen table or a quiet desk somewhere, try to keep the venue the same. Not only does this trick our brains into getting ready, it also helps to establish a positive habit.
- *Set a timer.* This may seem silly but it really works. You need to ask yourself how much time you can spend, right then and there, on marking. Be realistic. If it is more than 30 minutes, set the timer for a 30-minute chunk, then take a five minute break before setting it again. The use of a timer, like the choice of a specific marking spot, trains our brains and bodies, and creates a good habit. Try it. It really works. If at the end of the time period, or several time periods, you are not finished, leave the rest of the marking for another time. When you know you are going to work for just 30 minutes, it's amazing how much you can get done.
- *Assume the marking stance.* Rather than feeling annoyed, grumpy, or even angry that you have to spend a chunk of your precious time marking, think positively! You are fortunate to be able to share the growth of young people. You have an extremely important role in their lives. You are lucky to be the one to give them valuable feedback and direct their lives. Mentally applaud yourself and smile.
- *Avoid interruptions.* Tell others around you not to disturb you. Don't bring a phone or any other device to your marking corner. Put everything on hold for a little while. (Remember, you are only working in 30-minute chunks!)
- *Choose a marking strategy.* If this has not been established ahead of time (e.g., using a rubric), quickly decide how you are going to mark (see pages 132 and 135). Stick to your decision and mark all papers/projects/tests the same way.
- *Be realistic.* Know how much you really can accomplish at one sitting. Pushing yourself past this point doesn't help you or the students, so learn to establish your personal boundaries.
- *Divide and conquer.* Divide the marking into manageable bundles. Use a file system or baskets and divide the papers/projecs/tests into bunches. It is easier to attack a small bundle than an enormous pile. This is a sort of brain trick, because eventually you will have to mark the enormous bundle, but attacking it in smaller piles really does make it seem like less work.
- *Do a quick skim:* Start with a quick skim of all or several papers to get a feel for overall class level of performance. This could mean skimming (and then marking) one question at a time, the same question on each paper.
- *Keep a grade book:* Keep a book or spreadsheet specifically for grades and comments, and record as you go, not when all the marking is finished. Keep notes of common errors to return to at a later date.
- *Use points comments:* Consider using a set of comments attached to numerical points. This allows for speedy marking and provides a bit more than just a check or an X. The comments might look like this:

5 – Excellent
4 – Very good
3 – Good but needs some work
2 – Some problems to work on
1– Some difficulties. Please see me.

Obviously you would not use this system all the time, but for speedy, once-in-a-while marking, it can be effective.

- *Use a Comments Bank:* Find and use a good comments bank. There are many online. My only suggestion is to remember that, even when students' names are entered into the comments bank, it still feels a bit impersonal. You can supplement the bank comments with a short personal comment of your own.

## Marking Objective Work

The focus here is not on electronic marking, although most of the suggestions apply to this as well, but to marking by hand. The old, tried-and-true check-and-star method is still effective, but is not necessarily efficient in terms of time. Here are some tips and techniques for more efficient and speedy marking. Before you begin marking work that is highly objective—e.g., multiple choice, true/false, short-answer questions with only one right answer—ask yourself why you are marking it. Students learn from feedback, sure, but couldn't they mark these themselves? Or mark peers? Delegating this task would greatly reduce your marking time and leave you more time to evaluate the longer, more-subjective student work. If, however, you must mark this type of work, here are a few tips.

> Of course, these strategies can be used for more subjective marking, like longer literacy papers, but are especially suited to objective, short-answer projects.

- Stamp It: Purchase a small stamp pad and a couple of stamps, one that will indicate *Correct* and the other *Incorrect*. Be sure to show students your stamps and explain their purpose.
- Parts Mark: This means marking only selected portions of work. This saves time and makes students very aware of what they are doing; they don't know exactly what will be marked. Tell students you will be marking some, but not all, of the questions. In this way you can give proper attention to the portions marked; since students don't know what portions will be marked, they work equally hard on all. You might, for example, mark every other question, or every third question. If, when doing this, you notice a student is having difficulty, that is the time for a more in-depth look.
- Initial It: Initial what you mark. Sometimes initialing can indicate you have checked to see the work was done, but have not actually corrected it. This method is often used with homework; it insures that the work is completed, and you and the student can mark it together or in any other way you decide. It is possible to get a stamp made of your signature or initials; this speeds up your work and gives an official feel that students love. Just skim and initial. Avoid initialing without explaining to students what your initials mean. I once saw a student's paper with initials on it, and most of the answers were incorrect. When I questioned the student, he told me, "Teacher initialed it so it must be right." Your initials have to say a little more than that you simply saw the paper. You don't have to mark it all, but if you notice a mostly incorrect paper, you need to follow up.
- Individual Assessment: This means each student marks their own work. It is commonly used for marking simple, objective response work. Although it has

the merit of students immediately seeing their own mistakes, they tend to dislike it, and frequently get bored and mark inaccurately. You still need to do a quick check yourself when students mark their own work. In addition, students who are self-marking require a marking key that is completely objective; e.g., basic math facts or spelling words. Advise students they will be self-correcting and share the manner of correcting (you call the correct answers, students refer to answer sheet, etc.). Remind them of the importance of checking properly. Be present and visible while they are correcting.

- Seek and Find: This refers to quickly marking work but not putting any marks on the page. Simply indicate the number of correct responses (indicating the number wrong is less motivating), and students locate and correct as many wrong answers as they determine from the total minus the correct answers. Keep a running list of errors and good points. Mark this at the tops of pages, and be sure to record results in your marks book.
- Color Underlining: This is a quick and surprisingly effective method of drawing student attention quickly to right and incorrect responses by underlining various parts of the paper in different colors. Use two pre-established colors. Underline words/sections/responses that are good in one color; underline words/sections/responses that are not-so-good and need some improvement in another. If you wish, a third color can indicate a response you want to see again for re-marking.
- Peer Marking: Although commonly used, and despite the fact that this can be time-efficient, peer marking is fraught with potential difficulties. It is generally assumed that students learn from marking each others' work. However, too often they view it as boring busywork, and mistakes are easily made. My suggestion is to save this form of marking for occasional use. When you do use it, constantly change who is marking whose work. Explain what is expected of the students in clear, concise words and examples. Be sure they understand the procedure and advise them to mark neatly as they would want their own paper marked.

## Marking Written Work

This is where the element of time becomes very real. Marking stories, essays, and reports can take hours of teacher time, leading to teacher fatigue and frustration, which, in turn, does not make for good marking. Yet this marking is exactly the sort of feedback students need to move ahead. Keep in mind that students have put a lot of time and effort into the work; they deserve your time and effort in looking at it. By providing thoughtful feedback, you are building bridges for your students and giving them tools to better themselves.

1. Identify Purpose: Mark with purpose. Know exactly what you are looking for; e.g., perfect sentence structure, good grammar, correct spelling, specific content related to another subject, or evidence of problem-solving technique. If you identify what you are looking for, and share this with students while they are writing and creating, marking will be more time-efficient. Of course, you will quickly scan the rest of the work, making hasty notes on other areas that need to be dealt with at a later time. Basically this is checking to see if your lesson objectives are being met. Jot down your objective(s) in visible point form and check them with each paper you mark.

2. Be Aware of Bias: Watch for these two kind of bias.

- Presentation Bias: This is exactly what it sounds like—an innocent partiality against a paper/report/etc. that is not as tidy, clean, and/or visually appealing as another one. Keep in mind that not all students are created equal, and the less-visually appealing paper may, in fact, be superior in content. Just be conscious of what you are looking for in the papers.
- General Bias: I know as teachers we try very hard not to be prejudiced, but we are human, and biases can interfere with even the best intentions. Just being aware that the demon of prejudice can rear its ugly head when we are marking can help us keep it in check. We might face this situation when student-chosen topics do not sit well with us, when student arguments are different from our own, when students take stances we disagree with, etc. Remember that teacher are the models of society; be a nonbiased role model. Just stay aware of your own personal biases. We all have them, but they have no place in teaching.

3. Avoid Middle Marking: The tendency to "mark to the middle" is very real. This refers to the undesirable tendency to mark everything *good* or *fair*, with no real *excellent*s or *poor*s. Sometimes teachers middle mark unwittingly. But being aware of this tendency will help you avoid it; it also is helpful to constantly check back to see that not all your marking is the same.

4. Consider Assignment Objectives and Focus: I know that the temptation is to mark every piece of written work in detail. But remember that you have 20 to 30 more papers to mark. In-depth marking usually lasts for the first few papers, then fatigue takes over. So instead, mark selectively, looking only at the criteria initially shared with the students. Just mark it! If while doing this you note specific areas of weakness or concern, keep a running record for later teaching.

5. Personalize: Think of marking as if was a conversation between yourself and the student. Use their name in your comments, and use comments that reflect your knowledge of the student, as this is motivating to them. Write at least one comment that is specific to each student exclusively. This is not as hard as it sounds. Here are some examples:

   *Dom, your writing shows me how much you…*
   *Shana, your love of _____ shines through because…*
   *Jazmyn, I can see you want to…*

6. Mark Unobtrusively: I will never forget the student who once said dejectedly, "There are so many red marks on my essay that I can't even read it any more." Use a pencil to write comments and suggestions. Compared to ink, it is less invasive, easier to correct if you change your mind about a comment, and gentler on the student.

7. Use Positive Reinforcement: Be sure to add more positives than suggestions for change. Praise something the student has done effectively, especially if it's related to the specific area the assignment focuses on. Sometimes the focus area is too weak to praise; in this case, praise something else. Once I actually had to write, "I'm glad to see you put your name correctly in the bottom right." Use specific vocabulary to identify what is good and why. Whenever praise is given, to be effective it must be specific. "Good work," isn't enough. What is good? What is work in this case? Instead try comments like these:

Of course, every word you write on a paper takes time, so you might want to simply use the a comment where you simply choose an adjective and fill in the aspect you are commenting on: Better/excellent/improving/needs work _____ (grammar, sentences, verbs, character development, etc.)

Great job of…
I like how you…
Excellent use of…
Thanks for sharing your wonderful…
Your _____ is/are much better than last time.
I am happy to see…
It's great the way you…
I can see you worked hard on…

8. Take Immediate Action: Get to the marking sooner rather than later. Don't put it off. It is a major component of your professional responsibility, not something to be ignored or done hastily. In addition to it being your ethical duty, there are other important reasons to mark student work correctly and with thought. Marking is not just busy work! Consider: marking provides immediate feedback to you regarding how well a student is doing or what areas are in need of more work. And marking serves as both reinforcement and motivation for students.

## Giving Feedback

- Challenge students by gently pushing them with phrases such as

  Next time, why not add…?
  This is good. Now consider taking it a bit further and…
  I like your use of _____. You could use even more if you…

- Tell students specifically how to improve. Even the good ones. For example:

  If you add _____, you will be able to…
  You need to use a thesaurus to…
  Remember to use sentence variety and…

- Check your notes to see if students have followed up on any comments you have made previously and react accordingly.
- Focus on improvement. Use specific phrases, such as

  This is so much better than _____ because…
  You have improved your…
  I can see you are working on…

- Provide two positives for every negative. Limit the negatives or suggestions for improvement to two or three.
- Consider thanking students for sharing their work. Writing is a very personal experience. Think how pleased each student would be if they found the comment, "Thank you for sharing this beautiful piece about…" on a paper.
- Be aware that too much marking can actually prevent students from using self-regulation strategies like editing and proofreading.

> "True teachers are those that use themselves as bridges over which they invite their students to cross; then, having facilitated their crossing, joyfully collapse, encouraging them to create their own bridges." — Nikos Kazantzakis

## Strategies for Marking Written Work

### USE EXEMPLARS

Exemplars are examples of finished projects, paragraphs, papers, etc. that you have either created or borrowed (with permission) from students. They are meant for use in grading and consequently to improve other students' work.

Students can be given copies to criticize and evaluate alone, with peers, or as a class. Exemplars are excellent learning tools, as well as indicators of various levels of achievement. If you do not have exemplars available (for example, curriculum content), you can approach the literacy department of your educational system to request them. Or you can use students' work. Or you can generate examples of both good and bad work yourself. I like this last approach as it allows me to focus on exactly what I want in any given project. For example, if I am teaching use of vivid descriptors in a paragraph, I can write a paragraph filled with active verbs and colorful adjectives, and another paragraph that makes overuse of the words "nice" and "good" as descriptors.

### GOOD AND NOT-SO-GOOD

This is a strategy that makes students look critically at their own work to select what they think is good and what they think might need improvement. It is a helpful marking strategy, as it gives you somewhere to start. You can agree/disagree with what students have chosen and go from there. This can save time, as you may choose not to mark the entire piece, but instead to focus only on what the student has selected. Tell students that, once they have finished a final draft, they are to check their work for the two salient assessments and to write one sentence about each, telling what parts they have selected and why.

### RUBRICS

You are no-doubt familiar with use of a rubric, an assessment tool that indicates expected achievement criteria. A rubric is a set of rules, boundaries, or grids that simplifies marking. In other words, it is a scoring tool that explicitly represents the performance expectations of a piece of work. There are holistic, analytic, and developmental rubrics, the details of which can easily be found online. For the purposes of this book, I will refer to rubrics in general. Use of a clearly designed rubric definitely simplifies and expedites your marking.

Why use a rubric?

- reduces marking time
- specifies content being examined
- helps students focus on specifics
- clarifies expectations
- allows for easier peer marking or self-assessment
- helps students understand assignment guidelines
- is motivating and empowering for students

There are many rubric templates online. Find one you like and use it frequently. Keep a blank template always available for quick access. You can fill it in in moments, and use technology to share.

1. Decide on specific criteria you and/or students want to see in the project. Limit the number of criteria depending on age/abilities of students. Often two criteria are sufficient.
2. Consider involving students in the rubric creation. This increases accountability and student sense of ownership. When you involve students in developing the guide, it becomes harder for them to slack off, because they have identified their own needs and understand the expectations early, before they actually begin the work.

Rubric co-development can also be useful when explaining a not-so-good mark to parents. When a child explains that they were using a scoring tool they helped develop, there is little room for argument.

3. The rubric can be as short or long as you want, but keep in mind that short and specific will make for quicker marking.
4. Include expected levels of achievement that can just be circled to save time.
5. Describe criteria in detail, breaking each down into several easily accessible parts. For example, for the criterion of Sentence Structure, details could include

- variety in length
- variety in types of sentences
- correct sentence structure; e.g., no fragments/run-ons

## SUMMATIVE ASSESSMENT

The word assessment has Latin roots from *assidere*, which means "to sit beside."

Students should never read feedback on summative assessments. It is much more effective if you provide that feedback while the student is working on the paper/project/assignment or not at all. Sit with the students who are struggling the most; sit with them the most often.

## PEER SHARE

This is an activity that is less actual marking and more personal development, but I have included it since you can use it as a sort of formative evaluation. It is an activity in which students circulate and take turns looking over the shoulders of peers to check the work and offer suggestions. Allow a few students at a time (five or six) to circulate while others are writing, to read and react to their peers' work. This system takes a bit of training, and you need to remind students of the specific goal of the writing. Students critique each other's work, and learn by doing so.

## DELAYED MARKING

Using this strategy, you look at students' work as they work and even after its completion, giving verbal or written feedback but not assigning a grade until a later point. Unfortunately this is not a time-efficient procedure, as it requires a lot of teacher time, but it is very effective when you want students to work at revising, improving, and editing their work. Set up a time during the day when you can see students individually for no more than 10 minutes each to look at their work with them. This might be during a silent reading or writing time, it can be pre- or post-school or at a break if necessary.

## TWO-SIDED DISCUSSION

This marking strategy can be used at any point in the writing or project-creation process. Student and teacher have a quick face-to-face, in which the student shares concerns, dislikes, frustrations with the current task. The other students know not to interrupt when you are conducting these discussions since they will each have a turn. This works well to help students who are stuck or not performing up to par. Students appreciate this chance to air grievances or get help. Tell the class that you will be doing two-sided discussions for the next while and cannot be interrupted. Move to the students or have them come to you at a designated spot in the room. Open by asking them what they are finding the most troublesome or difficult with what they are doing.

## CLASS CONTRIBUTIONS

In this strategy, each student presents their writing or project to the class as a whole. The class responds with positive comments and suggestions. Students can be quite cruel to each other, so measures must first be taken to teach them how to respond effectively but kindly. Once this has been done, students can and will be experts.

1. Model critique of a piece of work.
2. Draw names randomly or ask if any student(s) wants to begin the activity. You might have a few who love to go first. Help the class respond by using leading questions, such as

> What did you like about…?
> Have you any suggestions for…?
> Is there something you would change about…?
> How did it make you feel to…?

### LAST WORDS ON MARKING

- Your fatigue is a factor. Your marking can and does change as you tire. Solution? Use a timer.
- Be aware of prejudice, either in presentation or content. Remember what is really important in what you are evaluating.
- Reset your mood frequently. Try to maintain the attitude that marking is not drudgery but a privilege. As your mood changes, so does your marking. Solution? Keep reminding yourself how important your marking is, and how fortunate you are to be in such a rewarding position in life.
- Avoid ranking students in a place they can see. I appreciate that you need to do this for reporting, etc. But students themselves do not need to be told who is first and who is last. They manage enough of that on their own. Instead, model acceptance of all and appreciation of something from everyone.
- Avoid generalities like "good" or "not-so-good" that really mean nothing at all. Be very specific with everything you write or say. Focus on some exact point, stance, or inaccuracy in the student's and work from there.

## The Wow of Teaching

**How-to-Wow of Being a Teacher**
- **Motivate students.**
- **Know curriculum content.**
- **Be a leader.**
- **Be a confident role model.**
- **Maintain a tidy classroom.**
- **Continually upgrade with professional development.**
- **Be forever patient.**
- **Have a sense of humor.**

Teaching is a multifaceted profession; I doubt anyone could list all the varied responsibilities it entails. And all those commitments and obligations come with specific deadlines. Consider this abbreviated list of teacher responsibilities—a teacher must: motivate students, deliver instruction, have an in-depth understanding of content, help students develop strategies for life, have an awareness of student diversity, be a behavior manager, be a leader, be a role model, be involved in ongoing professional development, and have a good sense of humor. And these are just a few of the main roles that come to mind. Luckily, many of the necessary traits of each role are common to most or even all of them. Here, I will offer a few how-tos for some of these many teacher responsibilities. It is important to note that any and all of the following skills, traits, or abilities can be taught to your students as well as to yourself, but that this section is primarily geared toward teacher self-improvement.

Teaching is a huge undertaking with far-reaching responsibilities, but exciting in its reach. The wow of teaching is what makes it fun for both teachers and students, and if you have done everything you can to make the learning experience meaningful, exhilarating, and stimulating, you have unlocked the mystery of the wow.

## Motivating Students

"It doesn't matter how slowly you are going as long as you don't stop." — Confucius

There are many books strictly about motivation (my *3-Minute Motivators* being one), so only a brief summary will be offered here. The old cliché *You can lead a horse to water but you can't make it drink* applies here. It is impossible to make students work, and even more impossible to make them learn, if they don't want to. However, it is a teacher's responsibility to keep trying.

1. Maintain a positive, excited, enthusiastic attitude. Your passion for a topic is motivating.
2. Be prepared. Winging it is seldom motivational
3. Set and share realistic goals. Keep them very visible.
4. Use a variety of teaching strategies (see Chapter 2). Keep mixing them up. Avoid being predictable.
5. Use action-based motivational tricks; get students up and moving for a few seconds per lesson.
6. Use examples and anecdotes. Let students see how they will benefit from the learning.
7. Praise freely; criticize constructively. Don't overuse either, and use both specifically.
8. Give students a sense of control over their learning/work; offer choices.

## Being a Teacher-Leader

"If your actions inspire others to dream more, learn more, do more, and become more, you are a leader." — John Quincy Adams. I would respectfully change the final word to "teacher."

Ask any teacher if they are a leader and most will probably have to think before responding. In fact, every teacher is a leader, even those who present a timid, quiet demeanor to the world. Every day, you are a leader in your class. Students listen to your every word, even when sometimes they appear to be doing otherwise. They watch your movements and mimic your expressions. They take to heart your likes and dislikes, and feel your passion for some subjects more than others. A leader is, by definition, one who takes charge in the direction of others, but often the best leadership skills look a lot like followership skills. Good teacher-leaders will, for example, often make themselves vulnerable by asking for feedback from students and/or peers. This, in turn, promotes conversation and collaboration, both goals of a good leader. That's you! A good leader! With that knowledge comes great responsibility. You must always act like a leader.

1. Maintain integrity. Being honest and trustworthy, and having strong moral principals—these are all components of integrity, and integrity is, perhaps, the most important leadership quality a teacher can possess.
2. Employ excellent communication skills.
3. Be passionate and committed. Your passion as a teacher will be what makes students motivated, and your commitment to their development and well-being is what keeps them motivated.
4. Be innovative and resourceful. As a teacher-leader, you have to think on your feet. You have to constantly be alert to everything that is going on around you, and able to react instantaneously.
5. Collaborate with others. Your leadership role in teaching demands that you collaborate well and frequently with others. This doesn't mean just colleagues, although they are the primary collaborators, but also parents, principals, and community members. Your ability to cooperate and affiliate, always with an open mind, is a necessary leadership quality.

6. Understand and appreciate curriculum. It goes without saying that good teacher-leaders know their curriculum. The curriculum is a teacher's bible; it should always be present and evident in everything taught in the classroom.

7. Be positive. In this case it is better to be a Pollyanna than a sourpuss. The famous Monty Python song tells you to "always look on the bright side of life." This is a good mantra for a teacher-leader. No one wants to follow a grumpy or negative person. No one *will* follow such a person. And since you are a teacher, and therefore a leader, use your teacher face even when you don't feel like it.

## Being a Role Model

"Like a fine flower, beautiful to look at but without scent, fine words are fruitless in a man who does not act in accordance with them."
— Buddha

A role model, at first glance, seems not unlike a leader, but there are a few subtle differences. Remember that children are expert imitators, and their teachers are the ones they imitate the most. You, their role model, have the responsibility not so much to *tell* them how to live, but to *show* them. The essence of being a good role model is acting in accordance with our words. There are numerous points that could be cited for being an effective teacher role model, but I have culled them to the ones I know work the best.

1. Be humble. No one likes arrogant people who think primarily of themselves. Put others, your students certainly, first. Avoid the temptation to boast or brag, even if the situation seems to call for that. If you have a student who fits the description *arrogant*, be even more humble around them. Model by example.

2. Be organized and on time. Students often have difficulty with organization. Have you checked a backpack lately? Model good organizational strategies (see Chapter 3). Demonstrate good organization by packing/unpacking your briefcase/backpack in front of them (you don't have to talk about it, just do it), and by maintaining an organized desk. Point out how important being on time is with statements like, "It's great that we are all here on time because…"

3. Demonstrate generosity, tenderheartedness, and acceptance of others. Students are often quick to reject those who are different. Your acceptance and appreciation of all students, and all people, will go a long way to modeling more appropriate behavior.

4. Demonstrate the ability to problem-solve and overcome obstacles. When things go wrong, and they will, make a point of modeling and talking about good problem-solving practices. Teachers have to be spontaneous; it's the nature of the job. But students are more likely to explode or have meltdowns when things go terribly wrong. So when something goes wrong with your plans, make it a teachable moment and talk through how you will solve the problem or remedy the situation. A Grade 3 teacher had planned an exciting art lesson in the use of clay, and the students were primed to create Mother's Day objects with the medium. They had had lead-up lessons in how to manipulate the clay, what kinds of objects were best, etc. But when the teacher opened the box, the clay was rock hard. Apparently there had been a small hole in the plastic wrap and the clay had completely dried out. Disaster! Quickly the teacher asked the students to work in pairs to figure out why the clay was dry (they had not yet discovered the hole) and to write a sentence of explanation, while she raced to the supply room to grab something else they could work with. The something else turned out to be colored paper and craft

sticks, which students put together to build small 3-D structures that were quite lovely in the end. As they were displaying their structures, the teacher asked the class if they had learned anything today and one student answered eagerly, "Not to blow your cool when things go wrong!" Success—on so many levels!

5. Look the part. Students notice every little detail of your physical appearance, so it really is important to look clean, tidy, and put together. One junior-high teacher wore long skirts. She had a genuine reason for this; she had one deformed leg. The students, however, were not aware of this. They simply saw her wearing lovely long skirts and before long many of the teenagers were also wearing long skirts, a fashion statement that existed nowhere but that particular school. Students see and copy. Or, if they don't copy, they acknowledge and file the information away. As a teacher, you are 100% visible every day. That means in the school community also. A Grade 1 student met her teacher in Safeway and exclaimed loudly, "*You* go to Safeway?" She was shocked that her teacher actually had a life that extended outside the school. But you do, and students never miss seeing you wherever you are.

6. Admit mistakes and accept consequences. We all make mistakes, but children often immediately turn to blame or feigned innocence when confronted with a blunder they have made. The best way to help them understand the significance of admitting to one's mistakes is to make a point of openly admitting to yours. Even little mistakes are perfect teachable moments. Use phrases like, "We all make mistakes," "It's human to be wrong sometimes," "I accept the consequences of…" While teaching history, a teacher said that buffalo and bison were from the same family and were the same size. The next day a student came with the news that his dad had said buffalo were actually larger than bison. The teacher immediately researched, found the student to be right, and took steps. She pointed out how she had spoken without enough evidence, how she was wrong, and what she was going to do about it. She wrote a note to the father thanking him for correcting her error, and apologized to the class.

"One important key to success is self-confidence. An important key to self-confidence is preparation."
— Arthur Ashe

7. Be confident; be yourself—positive, calm, self-assured. If you are thinking, *But I am not confident*, please take the time to reassure yourself that you are a teacher and you are, therefore, a confident person. Find ways to develop and support your confidence.

   - Think positive. When a situation calls for thought, consciously stop the pessimistic thoughts and force positive ones into your mind instead. You can do this. It is a matter of will. Maintain a *I think I can* mentality.
   - Push your limits. When you think you can't do something, stop and tell yourself you can at least try. Whether you succeed or fail, the act of trying boosts confidence.
   - Be curious. Develop an active mind that, instead of being passive, is always questioning situations and occurrences. Be aware of new ideas and new directions. The busier your mind is with unique ideas, the more confident you will be.
   - Identify areas of self-doubt. We all have these, but confident people deal with them effectively by taking the time to self-question. Ask yourself why you have self-doubt and what barriers are stopping you from overcoming it. Once you have found those barriers, make a point of removing them. Talk this out with a confidant if it will help. Remember that you alone are stopping yourself, and that you alone can push yourself forward.

## Dealing with Parents

"It's a funny thing about parents. Even when their own child is the most disgusting little blister you could ever imagine, they still think he or she is wonderful." — Roald Dahl

For some lucky teachers, meeting parents, especially for the first time, is easy. For all the rest of us, here are some helpful hints. First off, there are some things to be aware of and always remember:

- Parents are as nervous about meeting you as you are about meeting them.
- Parents have great love for their children and usually believe they are perfect, no matter what evidence there might be to the contrary.
- Parents want you to be perfect for their children.
- Parents want to hear only good things about their children; the not-so-good things will cause them distress.
- Parents are people too, human beings with flaws and weaknesses, but most truly want what's best for their children.
- Everything you say can and will be remembered; be careful of words that once spoken cannot be taken back. Think before you speak!

So, then, how *do* you meet and greet parents? Is there some magical formula to follow no matter whether the student in question is succeeding or failing? Yes, there is. Do your homework before the initial parent/teacher conference:

1. Know exactly what you want to convey to the parent(s).
2. Have concrete evidence with you; i.e., examples of student's work.
3. Find out what you can about parents before the initial conference. This is especially important if you have troubling information (behavior concerns, low grades, lack of motivation, etc.) to share.
4. Ask the child's previous teachers about them.
5. Check school registration forms to see if anything untoward is happening at home; e.g., recent divorce, foster care, etc.
6. Ask your principal for any available information.
7. If possible, find out the vocation of the parent(s). You may be able to use this as an in during the conference.
8. Definitely learn correct name pronunciation, especially if the names differ from that of the student.

### Parent/Teacher Conferences

At the time of the first parent/teacher conference, whether students are involved or not, know that there are effective and appropriate ways to handle this potentially stressful situation. It seems that no matter how experienced a teacher is, parent conferencing and/or meeting can be challenging. But you can meet the challenge with poise and confidence.

1. Avoid sugar-coating negatives. Parents deserve your candor. If a student is struggling, failing, or misbehaving, the parents have a right to know. It's human nature for them to want to hear only good stuff about a child, but it is your professional responsibility to be honest.

   - Begin with a positive statement about the child in question.
   - Open a discussion with the assumption that the parents probably already know about the problematic situation, using phrases such as

     "You are probably aware that _____ is struggling with…"
     "I do have one concern to share with you…"

Parents look to you to be the best possible mentor and educator of their children as possible. Do not misplace their trust.

"There is an area of concern in _____'s work/behavior/attitude that I'd like us to talk about."

**How-to-Wow Parent/Teacher Conferences**
- **Meet pleasantly, using names correctly.**
- **Share a positive.**
- **Get right to the point (positive or negative).**
- **Listen, listen, listen!**
- **Review and summarize.**
- **Close on a positive note and with sincere thanks.**

- Wait for a few seconds and evaluate the parent(s) response. Remain assertive, but listen carefully to them and let them finish what they have to say. In other words, keep in mind what you want to accomplish—the establishment of a plan to deal with the problem.
- Direct the discussion towards problem-solving. Be sure to come with at least one idea yourself, but ask for parental input.
- Close by summarizing the discussion and once again sharing the plans for the child.

2. Use the 4 Ps of Parents rule: be Polite, Professional, Pleasant, and Prompt.

- Polite: Remember your manners with parents, even if they frustrate you, annoy you, or simply seem to refuse to listen. They are concerned about their child and that is probably all that matters to them. Remember your manners!
- Professional: No matter what happens, remember that you are a professional, and with that comes professional ethics and a moral code. Under no circumstances should you discuss other students or issues other than the status of the student in question. You are not there to be the parents' friend. You are the conscientious educator of their child. Be professional!
- Pleasant: You are the one in control of the conference. Set a standard by smiling and being pleasant. This will help put anxious parents at ease and will make you feel more relaxed. The familiar expression "fake it until you make it" comes to mind. Remain pleasant even if you have to convey less-than-pleasant information. You can be serious and still be pleasant.
- Prompt: I cannot stress enough the importance of being prompt and not keeping parents waiting. Our lives involve too much waiting already. Teachers are known and respected for their promptness (you cannot be late when an active class is waiting!). For your parent/teacher conferences, vow to eliminate waiting altogether. If you have 10 minutes scheduled per parent, and time is up but you have not brought the meeting to an acceptable conclusion, tell the parent(s) that time is up and immediately reschedule another appointment. Avoid telling parents you will call later to set up another time, as this leaves them feeling unfulfilled. Always be prompt!

## Communicating Negative Information to Parents

Conferencing is easy when the student is doing well and there is nothing untoward to report. But what about the opposite situation? Sometimes it is necessary to share information with parents that is not particularly what they want to hear. Everyone wants to hear how well their children are doing, so communicating anything else can be tricky. In fact, it often feels easier to ignore the situation entirely. However, it is your professional responsibility to let parents know, to the best of your ability, if, how, and when students are struggling in any way. This, of course, includes if they are struggling socially, emotionally, intellectually, or in the area of motivation and/or work ethic.

1. Welcome the parent(s) by name, focusing on what you have in common—their child: "You are the parents of _____."

2. Avoid small talk. The parents are probably aware that some less-than-good news is coming and are anxious, so get right to the point.

3. First share something positive, even humorous, related to the student.

4. Begin the rest of the conference using phrases such the following:

   "As you know, _____ is struggling in…"

   "Although your child is trying, _____ is having a hard time with…"

   "_____'s work in _____ needs our attention."

5. Wait for a response and/or reaction. Keep in mind that all good communication involves even better listening. Parents may share information that explains or clarifies a situation, or they may be overwhelmed and unsure of what to do. It is your professional responsibility to appraise their responses or lack there of before proceeding.

6. Encourage input with questions such as

   "Are you aware of…?"

   "How does _____ behave at home?"

   "Has _____ shared this with you?"

7. Offer support. Recognize that they are feeling upset by using statements such as

   "This is upsetting news."

   "I can see you are concerned."

8. Open the discussion to possible solutions or remedies, being sure to listen to what parents say, as well as having some ideas of your own. This is where your homework counts. Never share a problem with parents without first thinking of at least one possible solution.

9. End the conference by first confirming the step/solutions decided upon, then finish off on a positive note. It is sometimes difficult to find a positive after a conference focusing on the negative. Here are a few ideas:

   "Let's not forget that _____ has a great sense of humor/ability to work hard/ desire to be better/home support system/etc."

   "I feel confident that together with _____, we can…"

   "Your input and concern has been very helpful to me. I think that within a few days/a week/a month we will notice an improvement in _____."

   "I appreciate your help in understanding _____. I am confident that we will/can…"

10. Remember to thank the parent(s) for coming and then quickly jot a few reminder-to-self notes before meeting the next parents.

There are many instances when the students themselves attend conferences, which then become goal-setting meetings with parents. If this is the case, it's important that students know ahead of time if you are going to share a problem or weakness with their parents. There should be no surprises. This allows students a chance to formulate a defense, and often they will have already come up with viable suggestions to share. In the case of parent/student/teacher conferences, the same steps apply, with the exception that you must continually ask for student input too.

## Managing Teacher Housekeeping

"You can't reach for anything new if your hands are still full of yesterday's junk." — Louise Smith

The amount of housekeeping required of teachers is quite amazing. Not only are there desks, lockers, tables, storage areas, backpacks, and closets, there is also the staff room (a place that simply craves clutter)—and all demand housekeeping. And let's not forget teachers' vehicles! The amount of stuff teachers require and pack around to facilitate student growth is astronomical. And it seems to multiply exponentially as the school year progresses. How can an already busy teacher cope? It is possible to declutter (see Chapter 3), to downsize, to minimize materials, and still teach very efficiently and effectively?

It is a true fact that life exists in entropy, a degree of disorder or uncertainty. Mess grows! A little chaos morphs quickly into a big chaos. But we can stop the progression if we take immediate action. If you want to give yourself a proverbial kick in the pants, watch a TV reality show about hoarding and I guarantee you'll be housekeeping that classroom immediately.

Use the same technique you use for decluttering a closet. If you haven't used an item for a year, and are not planning to use it very soon, toss it. By tossing I do not necessarily mean garbage it. There are other avenues to try first.

- Put items on a table in the hall with a *Free* sign for colleagues or parents.
- Offer to donate to local playschools, bible schools, teacher training programs, or neighborhood groups. Or have a school garage sale.
- Have someone (pay if you must; it's worth it) transfer all hard copy files, worksheets, etc. to digital format, then toss all the paper.
- Do a big clean-up. Many teachers come in early in September with the idea of doing a big housecleaning at that time, but find themselves bogged down with meetings, principal expectations, etc. Better to stay one day later in June and do the big toss at that time. Allow yourself a full day to minimize stuff. Keep in mind that less stuff means less cleaning, and that means less stress.
- Do a ten-minute-toss at the end of every day. Simply do a quick scan of papers and other things lying around and aggressively get rid of what has had its use. If you miss one day, treat it like taking a pill, and be conscientious about avoiding missing the next day. If you can't commit to every day, pick a few days and stick to them. Be vigilant with yourself. Ten minutes for a stress-free next day is well worth it.
- If you can't decide whether to keep something or toss it, toss it. Your indecision is your clue. Not sure? Don't need it. When something is really important to keep, you'll know it.
- Limit yourself to how much you are allowed to carry, spend, tote, store. Do not under any circumstances purchase more storage bins, shelves, or filing cabinets. The more places you have to store stuff, the more stuff you will hoard. And tell yourself that's what it is—hoarding!
- Remind yourself that a messy room is a sign of a messy person. Is this the image you want to give your students? Your principal? The parents?
- And what about the staff room? That is a shared responsibility, but you can lead by example by doing a great (not just good) job of clutter removing and housekeeping when it is your assigned day to do so.

## Professional Development

The world is changing rapidly and, with it, so is education. It is the responsibility of every teacher to keep up with all the changes not only in technology, but also in the ways in which human beings live on planet Earth. I know how tempting it is to quietly skip teachers' conventions, professional development days, and workshops and meetings. You are overworked; you have too much to do and no time in which to do it. But—and this is a very big but—it truly is mandatory that every teacher does their absolute best to stay current, to keep up with technology, ever-changing curriculum, subject knowledge, pedagogical and communication skills, social mores and values, and student interests and needs.

- Practice lifelong learning in your subject areas.
- Pursue continuing personal development. Attend every workshop, convention, conference, guest speaker, professional development activity, and class you can.
- Use the Internet with respect. Make use of everything, such as educational blogs, podcasts, e-books, social media pages, and relevant websites to continually upgrade your knowledge. Use social media.
- Use mentors who can help keep you up-to-date; mentor peer teachers by sharing new and novel ideas and information.
- Consider continuing education. Keep upgrading and taking courses. Don't be satisfied with the status quo. You expect excellence from your students, and they have a right to expect the same from you.

"Live as if you were going to die tomorrow. Learn as if you were to live forever. " —Mahatma Gandhi

## Developing Patience and Humor

### Patience

"One moment of patience may ward off great disaster. One moment of impatience may ruin a whole life." — Chinese proverb

I think we all agree that good teachers are patient—undeniably, unshakably patient. In fact, patience may very well be one of the most important characteristics of a teacher. The patient teacher is the one who displays an inner calm, even in the face of classroom chaos. The patient teacher is the one who is fully present in the situation, and is paying full attention to what is going on. Of course we'd all like to be this person 100% of the time, but in reality it's more difficult than it looks. And we'd like our students to be patient, too. This story reminds us that children are not automatically patient. A little girl attended Kindergarten for the first time, and after Day One her Nana asked her how Kindergarten was. The child answered solemnly, "Not good, Nana. They didn't teach me to read!" Obviously the patience required for learning to read had to be learned first. Being a patient child or adult is often hard work, but it is possible to become a more patient teacher.

1. Start each day with 60 seconds of silence during which you make the conscious choice to remain calm all day, regardless of what happens. Decide then and there that you will not lose your cool that day. It works!
2. Take about two more minutes to mentally prepare. Close your eyes and visualize your class, your students, your planned lessons, your activities all going smoothly. All together, steps 1 and 2 take only three minutes—time well-spent to boost your patience power.
3. If you feel things starting to escalate, remember your earlier choice, take several slow, deep breaths, and focus on your breathing for at least 60 seconds.

4. Speak and move slowly, more slowly than normal. Slow, even speech and slow movements have a calming effect on both you and your students.
5. At home or during free time create a Mindful of Triggers list. This is a list of situations that you know make you impatient. If possible, remove the stressors; if not possible, attack them one at a time (no multi-tasking).
6. Sometimes, make yourself wait; practice calming breathing while you wait. Good natural waiting places include medical offices, lines in stores and banks, the bus stop or airport waiting room. When you find yourself in one of these situations, it is a perfect time to practice calm waiting. Calm waiting is a skill, and all skills can be learned and honed.

## A Sense of Humor

Teaching is a tough job. It is demanding, exhausting, and often fraught with disappointment. And yet good teachers love their work. That is at least in part because they manage to maintain a great sense of humor; they have the ability to find enjoyment in all that they do. You may be wondering if you have a good sense of humor. You are a teacher, so I suspect you do but, just for fun, ask yourself the following questions and if you answer "yes" to all or most of them, you've got it! Do I...

- share jokes whenever I can?
- maintain a positive attitude (even when I'm not feeling it)?
- often make others laugh?
- enjoy watching comedies?
- enjoy sharing short, funny stories?
- see the humor in what children do?
- remain culturally and ethnically open-minded?
- use humor to defuse hot topics or situations?
- laugh at myself?

Chances are you have just admitted to having a good sense of humor, but if not, then perhaps it's time to develop that humorous component of your personality.

### HOW TO DEVELOP YOUR SENSE OF HUMOR

1. Review the list above; it contains the basics of good humor, and many of the points can be practiced and rehearsed consciously.
2. Train yourself to spot humor in everyday, mundane happenings. So you dropped your keys in the toilet. You can choose to be angry, or you can choose to see the humor in it, and, believe me, if you share that little story with students they will *really* see the humor.
3. Try to think of humor as a trump card to be played when a situation is nasty or headed in the wrong direction. Stop, take a breath, and find the funny. It's there. Be observant and creative, and use humor to defuse. Two male peer teachers who were known for getting on each other's nerves were arguing about the use of some equipment, and the altercation was becoming heated. A female teacher, watching calmly, suddenly grabbed two measuring sticks and handed them to the fighters, saying loudly, "And for today's fencing match we have Big Red in this corner and Hot Henry in the other!" Her quick thinking and sense of humor made everyone break into laughter. After feigning a quick sword fight, the two men abandoned the argument.

"Attitude is like a box of crayons that color your world. Constantly color your picture gray and your picture will always be bleak. Try adding some bright colors to the picture by adding humor, and your picture begins to brighten up." — Allen Klein
Let's all add more color.

"A person without a sense of humor is like a wagon without springs. It's jolted by every pebble in the road." — Henry Ward Beecher

4. Be skilled at language usage so that you can quickly pick up on play on words. Puns and double entendres only come to those with language mastery.

5. Work on maintaining a straight face when sharing a joke, amusing situation, or double entendre. Think poker face.

6. Have confidence in yourself and in your ability to make others laugh. This is not something that happens overnight; it takes time to cultivate a good sense of humor if you do not already have one. But you can take little steps all the time, by being alert to possible humorous situations and conversations, and by always thinking, *What's funny about this?*

7. Always be willing to laugh at yourself, and to share your personal blunders and gaffes.

8. Watch your students with a smile rather than a frown. Kids are funny! Look for their natural comicality. Instead of viewing their mistakes and blunders as upsetting, find the humor in them. Laugh with your students often and about everything. I know one teacher who kept a record of the amusing things her students said over the years of her career, and when she retired she wrote them into a book. I don't know if it was a bestseller, but it represented many years of laughter.

9. Watch stand-up comics, and comedy movies and YouTube shows. By immersing ourselves in comedy, we quite naturally improve our own senses of humor. So instead of watching that horror flick, choose funny.

10. Buy a couple of joke books or research jokes online; learn a few jokes from memory. If you do this regularly, you'll soon be looking forward to finding and sharing jokes with others. A fitness instructor always began her class with a relevant joke. One day she forgot the joke and after class several members commented on this. One even said, "The only reason I come to this class all the time is for the joke." Apparently humor can even make you fit!

"A day without laughter is a day wasted." — Charlie Chaplin

11. Play with humor. Ask students what's funny about a situation that might not seem funny at first. In a class of eager artists, an entire container of water was spilled accidentally, destroying the work of several students. This disaster was turned around when the quick-thinking teacher, hands on hips, said loudly, "Well, this is a mess. Every person who can tell me something hilarious about it can have five extra minutes at recess." The funny comments came fast and furious, and everyone, even the students whose projects were ruined, was laughing.

It's time to take the jump of faith and be more humorous. There are many ways to exercise a sense of humor, and not all work for everybody, so pick and choose from the following suggestions. Keep in mind the power of the laughter you will create, and then in turn, the power that will give you in the classroom.

- Consider your audience. What works with young children (e.g., knock-knock jokes) doesn't work with preteens or adolescents. With audience in mind, find a few joke books to keep on hand.

- When you decide to tell a joke, don't preamble or announce that you are going to tell a joke. Just jump right in and tell it, then wait. If it bombs, that's funny too, depending on your reaction. It then becomes a laugh-at-yourself situation and students will love that.

- If you are in the middle of what you thought was a funny story and it is bombing, stop and admit defeat. Say something like, "This was obviously funnier in my head than when I told it."

- Always use humor that amuses *you*. If you can't smile or laugh at it, no one else will. When searching for jokes or one-liners, check your own laugh meter first.
- Be a humor parrot. Parroting (copying of another comedian's material) is considered bad taste in the comic world, but for those of us who are not stand-up comics, there is no shame in parroting a pro. In fact, this is a good way for anyone not feeling very funny to get started. Copy the comedian's moves, mannerisms, timing, jokes. Human beings are masters at mirroring. Mirror a comic until you find your feet.
- Be witty, not sarcastic. Wit depends on spontaneity, which in turn depends on being alert and in the present. To be witty you need to combine innovative ideas almost instinctively. You can develop this ability by paying attention to witty people and by always thinking on the spot. It is even possible to practice wittiness (on a willing spouse or friend), and therefore to become more comfortable with it. The best way to improve wit is to be involved in verbal sparring with another individual who can give you honest feedback. You have to think quickly and keep your mind open to all possibilities.

### LAUGHTER IN THE CLASSROOM

You are probably thinking, "I am not a funny person. I don't have a great sense of humor." You are wrong. You are a teacher and all teachers are at least relatively funny or they wouldn't be able to manage the wear and tear of the profession. "Sense of humor" refers to the ability to see things in a humorous way, to appreciate and understand a joke, and to present oneself in a manner related to amusement and enjoyment. Think about yourself in the classroom. Have you ever seen things your students have done or not done as humorous? Have you at least occasionally told a joke in class, even if it was someone's refurnished joke? Do you, even sometimes, present yourself in a comic way and/or laugh at yourself with your students? Trust me when I tell you that you are an interesting and amusing person. Every day you stand (like a stand-up comedian) in front of a class of squirmy youngsters or hormone-raging teens, a captive audience, and have to somehow hold their attention. Surely you can see the humor in that? And that's where it begins.

"If we couldn't laugh, we'd all go insane." — Robert Frost

Overworked teachers may well be asking themselves why laughter is important in their classrooms when, surely, it detracts from focus on curriculum. Is it important? Let's look quickly at humor and laughter. We already know that laughter triggers endorphins and makes one feel good, but consider what else it does. It lowers blood pressure; decreases stress; increases muscle flexion and extension; promotes an overall sense of well-being; helps to shift one's perspective; increases circulation of antibodies in the blood, improving resistance to infection; builds positive relationships; and can even reduce pain. All that, with no side effects and no financial cost. These days, that's a miracle in itself! And aren't these positive results of a few giggles and chuckles exactly what we want in our classes? I believe, and have witnessed over and over again, that laughter in the class is the best indicator of a focused and functional atmosphere. And laughter is surely the wow we are seeking.

So if it is obvious that laughter is a tool that can and must be used in classrooms to facilitate conditions for learning, what about the teacher who struggles even to smile? If you feel you are just not funny, if you are uncomfortable telling a joke in class, or if you get embarrassed rather than being able to laugh at yourself, it's time to challenge yourself to a funny overhaul.

The following tips might help you show your funny side to your students in a non-threatening way. They are humorous actions as opposed to humorous talk.

- Draw funny little sketches/illustrations on work that you have marked. Simple things like happy/sad faces, eyes with tears, a big smiling mouth, etc. Think emojis. One middle-school teacher used to draw stick figures in various positions to show different levels of success of the work. Once, when a paper was done poorly, he drew a stick figure hanging by the neck with a very sad face; the student howled with laughter and redid the paper.
- Give messages in a humorous manner. One teacher wrote on the board before students arrived, "I know when you are copying from a neighbor. No one talks out of the side of their mouth and writes while looking straight ahead."
- Give feedback in humorous manner. A student somehow managed to complete only half of a math exam, and didn't hand in the other half at all. The teacher wrote, *Assuming the other half went missing in the Devil's Triangle.* Not only was this funny, but it also prompted the student to find out about the Devil's Triangle, which is similar to the Bermuda triangle but off the coast of Japan.
- Deliver an entire lesson (especially if it's mostly lecture format) in a weird mask or even complete costume. You don't even have to offer an explanation. If students ask, simply say you wanted to catch their attention, or you just felt like it.
- Think of ways to reply to a student's erroneous answer in an erroneous manner. For example, to the question "Why are there rings around Saturn?" a student answered "Because God liked it so he put a ring on it," to which the teacher wrote in response, "Saturn was not a single lady." (boredpanda.com)
- When creating a test or providing a written list, add one or two completely silly questions or comments. For example, on a spelling test a teacher asked for the spelling of *any word you want to spell*. On a science exam, one question was *What goes up when the rain comes down?* (an umbrella). On a homework to-do list, the third point was *Stand up, touch your toes, sit on the floor and spin around until you are dizzy.*
- Be on the lookout for amusing posters. They are everywhere. Just adding one to the classroom and changing it frequently adds an instant dash of fun.
- Respond to doodles that students write on papers, quizzes, etc. with a few comical words. For example, on strange alien doodle write, *Have you see them landing? Where?* On a doodle of a stick man write, *Love his outfit. Breezy and cool.*
- Occasionally let loose, laugh, make fun of yourself.
- Bring in humor from other sources such as short video clips, cartoons, funny memes or hashtags, YouTube videos. If they don't fit in with your objectives for the day, use them as quick comic-relief moments when the class is restless or bored.
- Add a dash of silliness to whatever you are doing. Keep in mind the interests of your students' age group and tie subject content to pop stars, super heroes, famous athletes, etc. For example, in the middle of a Grade 5 discussion about electricity and magnetism, casually throw in, "This is not the same magnetism as Connor McDavid (hockey player) has on the ice...or is it?
- Create a Funny Bones bulletin board and constantly post new humorous quotes, memes, cartoons, jokes, etc. Encourage students to bring humorous material for it also.

- One a month have a Humor Day and try to incorporate humor into every subject. Make the math problems funny (use students'/teachers' names). Have students write a funny narrative. Use joke books for reading. Read a humorous short story to students. Draw humorous cartoons, illustrations, etc. in art.
- Keep a class Humor Log in which every funny incident is recorded and, at random times throughout the year, revisit incidents and enjoy them all over again. There is a true tale of a very elegant teacher who honestly arrived in class with toilet tissue stuck to his shoe. The students tried to avoid laughing but finally gave in to hysterics. The wise and humorous teacher laughed right along with them and the Toilet Tissue Shoe incident was relived many times that year.
- Have a daily Tickle Time when each student in turn gets about two minutes to "tickle the fancy" of the other students with a joke, a riddle, a funny movement/ dance, etc. Have a good supply of joke/riddle books on hand for the student who forgets to prepare for their day.
- Regularly read to or share with your students funny poetry/short stories/news errors/etc. Search for material ahead of time and keep it handy. Try *A Bad Case of the Giggles* by Bruce Lansky or *Where the Sidewalk Ends* by Shel Silverstein. Older students (high school) may be thrilled by *Revolting Rhymes* by Roald Dahl (check it out yourself before reading aloud.)
- Have a Pun Party. Playing with words to appreciate the humor in puns is a higher-order thinking skill but, if the puns are simple enough, even the youngest students will enjoy them. Students may need a bit of coaching to understand, but they will still love the experience. At a Pun Party, each student must bring a pun and be prepared to explain why it is funny.
- Use Word Jumbles. These are problem-solving game activities. The humor lies in the solution. You can find them online at sites like http://www.jumble.com. There are a variety of games under the Jumble heading; they are worth a look if you have extra time for humor in your classroom.

No matter how you approach the use of humor, whether it's through the development of your own sense of humor or the addition of humorous activities in your classroom, you will be doing your students a real service. A good laugh overcomes fears and difficulties, and sets the stage for more productive activity. I will close this section with a wonderful quote by Dwight D. Eisenhower: "A sense of humor is part of the art of leadership, of getting along with people, of getting things done." All those qualities are essential for a teacher with wow—a teacher like you!

# Conclusion

After a survey of a variety of students, the following information came to light. When asked what made a teacher a "good teacher," the most common first response was "kindness." So it would appear, then, that all the worrying about how to teach means little without human kindness. I would agree, but would also encourage the following qualities as shared with me by students in this order of their importance: *sense of humor, honesty, trustworthiness, happy, enthusiastic, caring, energetic,* and *interesting.* Only after all these adjectives were provided in various manners, and after some subtle questions as to the teachers' abilities to actual teach, did the following words appear: "Knows the *stuff* she is teaching," "is fair," "is easy to understand," and "makes me want to learn." Say what you will, students know what they like. Nevertheless, a teacher who fits all or most of these qualities is most certainly one who has found the wow of teaching. This teacher is one who is always updating, improving, learning, and reading books like this one. So as a final word, I wish you all the wow in teaching.

## A Final Word about Wow

In today's world we are attracted to spectacular, the jaw-dropping, the stop-you-in-your-tracks scenarios. These are examples of the wow factor and certainly it seems that humanity requires more and more extremes to be wowed. In the class-room, however, where you have complete control, you can create a little wow every day if you simply keep this in mind: impress them somehow. Be prepared to disturb the status quo by introducing novel methods, interesting testimonials, child-centred stimuli, and unconventional approaches. Make everything you are teaching be the most important thing in the students' lives at that moment. Dazzle them with your enthusiasm. Excite all the senses and arouse curiosity. Make learning relevant—the more interesting and shocking the better. Even tiny, seemingly inconsequential facts or trivia related to what is being studied can wow students. Some teachers seem to be magic. They seem to be born with the wow factor. But creation of the wow factor can be learned, and it is a valuable learning that empowers teachers and students and is uplifting and rewarding to both.

# Index